Harbour Island

Fried Conch Fritters

Caprese Salad

Lobster
and Roasted Potatoes

Banana Pudding

Hotel Esencia

the beach

summer
clambake

7:30

Erin Lauder

...tes you to dinner
...to celebrate

RIN Beauty

...sday, March 28
7:30 pm

1000 Park Avenue

RSVP @ AERI...

...nder for dinner
...the newest AERIN fragra...

...at de Vert

...September 24, 2018
7PM

...Hôtel de Crillon
Salon des Aigles
...Place de la Concorde
...5008 Paris, France

Invitation non-transferable

Please Come
Celebrate Spring

Dinner
at Home

Saturday, April 6
7:30 pm

Ronald

ENTERTAINING BEAUTIFULLY

AERIN LAUDER
ENTERTAINING BEAUTIFULLY

Written with Jill Simpson
Principal photography by Simon Upton

RIZZOLI
NEW YORK

New York · Paris · London · Milan

To my mother, Jo Carole, and my grandmother
Estée, who taught me about elegance, attention to detail,
and the joys of entertaining family and friends.

Contents

Aerin and Eric

June 1, 1996

Beluga Caviar
Blini and Toast

Roast Chicken
Summer Vegetables
Mashed Potatoes

Watermelon Sorbet
~
Meursault-Blagny Premier Cru
Château de Blagny 1994
Louis Latour

Château Lafite Rothschild 1983
Pauillac

Dom Perignon 1988
~
Wedding Cake
and
Dancing, Dancing, Dancing

Introduction

I have always loved to entertain. Inviting people into one's home and hosting them for a meal is a gesture of generosity. It's so much more personal than going to a restaurant—it's warm and intimate, and it lets friends, family, and guests feel truly welcomed and cared for. I can trace my love of entertaining back to my childhood when my sister, Jane, and I would play for hours with our Barbie dolls and dollhouse. I would say, "There's a party tonight at my Barbie's house. Will you come?" and I'd tell her, "This is what we're going to serve. This is what everyone's going to wear." I would take control of the parties and my poor younger sister had to follow along. I also have fond memories of hosting tea parties with my grandmothers Estée and Sylvia in my nursery, with my miniature tea set and loyal stuffed animals.

I grew up surrounded by enchanting parties and dinners that inspire me to this day. I learned how to entertain from two incredible women: my grandmother Estée and my mother, Jo Carole. Both were flawless hostesses, but each had a different style. Estée entertained in a very formal way. She would have elegant, beveled gold-edged menus and place cards with calligraphy, matchbooks with her initials, and little gifts—like her glamorous compacts—at each place setting for the women. She had amazing collections of china and linens, some of which I've been fortunate enough to inherit.

My mother has great taste as well. Her table settings are enriched by her collecting, which includes American antiques such as spongeware, as well as European ceramics from the eighteenth through the twentieth centuries. She taught me the importance of crisply pressed linen napkins, polished silver, and sparkling glasses. Even now, when I host a special dinner, I'll ask her to come over and make sure I've set the table perfectly.

My first experience with my own formal entertaining was my wedding. Eric and I were married at my parents' home in the Hamptons on a picture-perfect June day. I wanted a traditional, elegant wedding in the country, with a romantic—but still luxurious—sensibility. As I was rather young at age twenty-five, my mother guided many of my choices, and in the process taught

My wedding truly was like a fairy tale. CLOCKWISE FROM TOP LEFT: Classic engraved menus echoed the invitations. I love this photo that captures my husband, Eric, and me after the ceremony. The cake by Sylvia Weinstock was adorned with pale pink sugar roses. Guests sat at long tables decorated with abundant bouquets of roses, many of them in my mother's silver and glass pitchers and bowls.

ELM

Dinner given by
The Lauder Family
in honor of
The Executives of
The Hanhausen–Douglas Group

Petite Marmite
Peached English Sole Veronique
Crown of Lamb Valencie
Heart of Bibb Lettuce
Brie
Baki

The "21"
Wed

To welcome back Chessy and Pat

Estée Lauder

requests the pleasure of your company
at a dinner party at the
la maison des champs
September 1st

Mr. and Mrs. Joseph H. Lauder
request the pleasure of your company

for dinner
on Friday, August 22nd
at eight o'clock

A Reminder
R.s.v.p.
Main Street, Wainscott
537-3920

Men: Jacket and tie
Women: short or long

me a great deal about how to plan a large-scale event. One thing I was very specific about was the kind of food I wanted—comfort food like roast chicken, mashed potatoes, and fresh vegetables—and that is still the kind of food I love to serve today. My mother introduced me to stellar professionals, many of whom I continued to work with for many years. Robert Isabell designed the breathtaking flowers, from my bouquet of lily of the valley to the profusion of pale pink roses and peonies at the reception, and Raúl Àvila, who often designs flowers for me now, worked for Robert back then. I was instantly taken with the impeccable elegance and warmth of Oscar de la Renta, whom I chose to design my wedding gown and the bridesmaids' pale blue dresses, and he became a close friend. Joy Lewis, of Mrs. John L. Strong, designed the classic engraved invitations and menus with a gilt edge and monogram.

The ceremony took place in an enchanted spot overlooking a pond and field of wildflowers, with a view of the ocean beyond. Afterward, we dined at long tables overflowing with roses and peonies nestled in silver and English glass vases and pitchers from my mother's collections. Those personal elements made everything more meaningful. My husband's uncle, John Barry, was a talented film composer and music was very much a part of Eric's upbringing, so we had the Orpheus Chamber Orchestra play during dinner; it was magical. Dessert and dancing afterward were in a separate tent, and true to my love of flowers (and sweets), our wedding cake, made by the incomparable Sylvia Weinstock, was covered in a cascade of pink sugar roses, crowned with a wickerlike basket of flowers, and the tables were filled with candies, cookies, and champagne. Usually when you get married young and look back, you find that your tastes have changed, but I would happily do it the same way all over again.

My wedding started a lifelong love affair with beautiful plates, linens, and glassware: I like to collect them when I travel and now I design them for my own collections. But I have definitely put my own more modern twist on the traditions I grew up with. I love to host an elegant dinner party, but there's also nothing I enjoy more than dinner on a tray in front of the TV. It might be takeout food eaten with chopsticks but it's still on a pretty tray with a linen napkin. I think entertaining can be done in all different ways. With three dogs and two sons who like to invite friends over at the last minute, my approach has to be spontaneous and relaxed.

Instead of gourmet, four-course meals, I prefer to serve comfort foods that people genuinely love to eat, from paella and a big salad in summer to savory roast chicken in the fall or dim sum on a Sunday evening.

Invitations from Estée's archives include everything from formal engraved cards and menus to handwritten ones.

Whether it's a special celebration in the office, a clambake in the country, or a cozy dinner with close friends après-ski, my starting point and the part I love the most is the table and the ambience. The spark of inspiration might be an alluring set of plates I discovered in Italy or treats from an amazing candy shop in New York City. It could be a place I've traveled to, a fabric I love, or the flowers growing in my garden that capture my imagination and serve as the catalyst for all the choices that flow from it.

I believe entertaining and table settings are truly a form of creative expression. When you put thought into the invitations you send, it establishes the tone and creates a sense of anticipation for the event. The table you set, the food and drinks you serve, the fragrance and beauty of the flowers all contribute to the alchemy of a wonderful evening. I love planning all those details, but I also never want it to feel too fussy or forced. The best entertaining, to me, is a mix of easy elegance and effortless chic. I think if you strive too hard for perfection, people can't relax and be themselves.

The secret ingredient of a memorable evening is the chemistry of the people you invite as well as the elements of spontaneity, warmth, and intimacy. Some of the most wonderful dinner parties I've ever been to took place in friends' kitchens, with everyone helping make the meal. And I've been to many formal dinners that unfortunately turned out to be stilted and boring. So my advice is to be true to yourself, aim for enjoyment rather than perfection, and leave room for serendipity. Let inspiration be your guide and laughter your measure of success.

I invite you to join me for a year's worth of my own entertaining at home, including an intimate supper in the city, a Halloween birthday party for my son, a springtime soirée in the country, and a picnic lunch on the water. I've also asked some of the friends whose style most inspires me to share a glimpse into their homes and parties. Maria Hummer-Tuttle welcomes guests to her refined Los Angeles home and Caroline Sieber von Westenholz hosts a whimsical Christmas celebration in London by way of her native Austria. My dear friend and decorator Daniel Romualdez entertains at his cozy antique farmhouse in Connecticut. And, of course, my list would not be complete without my parents' gracious New York homes. These are some of the style icons who have influenced me and generously shared their ideas and entertaining expertise.

I hope these ideas will inspire you to invite friends and family into your own home to celebrate the occasions that are meaningful to you, or just for the simple pleasure of sharing a meal and the company of friends. I promise that you'll find the rewards are well worth the effort.

My grandmother Estée at her formally set table in Palm Beach, Florida, where she spent winters. Her love of the ornate is evident in the crystal candelabra, cut crystal and gilded stemware, and intricate porcelain and ormolu accessories on the rococo mantel. I learned so much from her, but my tastes are decidedly more modern.

Make Time for Yourself

It may seem counterintuitive to begin a book on entertaining by focusing on a moment of solitude, but one thing I learned from my grandmother Estée is that it's worth taking the time to make any meal or occasion beautiful. Even when you're having your morning coffee or afternoon tea by yourself, it's deserving of a china teacup, cream and sugar served in a pitcher and sugar bowl, not a carton, and a linen napkin. These things only take a moment, but they elevate the entire experience, so that you can slow down and actually enjoy it. I find this kind of respite ever more important in our lightning-paced, tech-saturated modern world.

In our New York apartment, I am fortunate to have a sublimely feminine dressing room. It is my private refuge in a home filled with boys and dogs, and sometimes chaos and noise. Here in my secret garden, I can sip my coffee in the early morning before everyone else is awake, read on my chaise on a weekend afternoon, or take my time getting ready to go out in the evening. The walls are covered in a hand-painted Gracie wallpaper just like my grandmother had, with icy blue silk taffeta curtains with tasseled fringe and soft white wall-to-wall carpet. Though I have sisal on the floors in much of the rest of my home, here it's soft, quiet, and lovely to walk around in bare feet on the wool

In a way, this is my take on my grandmother's style. I have a similar hand-painted Gracie wallpaper in my dressing room, with touches of gilded furniture and luxurious silk curtains, but I find a monochromatic approach to be more modern and soothing. FOLLOWING PAGES: One wall is lined with closets and drawers, where I can hang whatever outfit I am wearing that evening. Enjoying a cup of tea from my elegant porcelain tea set before getting ready to go out helps reenergize me.

I think taking time for yourself is the secret to being a good hostess, wife, mother, and friend. I believe in putting the same care into a cup of afternoon tea for myself as I would when serving a guest. It's those little niceties that rejuvenate me.

carpet. Treasured notes and artwork from my children are framed on the wall, and sunlight streams through the large window. An afternoon cup of tea in my charming hand-painted teacup is often all I need to feel refreshed to tackle the rest of my workday or go out for the evening. This is also the place where I take a minute to relax before hosting a dinner or party. Enjoying a few moments of calm for yourself, so you can then truly focus on and enjoy your guests, is one of the secrets to being a good hostess.

Fresh flowers and your best china and silver shouldn't just be saved for special occasions or holidays: use them every day for yourself and notice the difference in how it makes you feel.

Drawings and notes from my sons when they were little are elegantly framed and given pride of place in my dressing room. They're as meaningful to me as the fine art in our living room, and much more personal.

SPRING

Spring feels like a time of new beginnings to me, even more so than New Year's. That first day you don't have to wear your heavy winter coat is so liberating and joyful. I find that the sunny, warm days of spring give me renewed energy to get out of my cocoon and entertain, whether we are in the city or country. Flowers are starting to bud in the garden and come into the market, from tulips and daffodils to grape hyacinth and lily of the valley. Soon, my favorites, such as peonies, lilacs, and roses, will be blooming. I love to walk outside in the country and cut branches of dogwood and Japanese magnolia to fill the house with the beauty and fragrance of spring. My palette becomes lighter, and I enjoy dressing my table with fresh floral patterns. All of a sudden, it feels like the perfect time to host a luncheon for my girlfriends or a dinner party. Spring is in the air—what more reason do you need to invite some friends over to celebrate?

Homage to Estée

Any time I want to recall how my grandmother entertained, I don't have to look very far. I inherited her house in the Hamptons, and although we've renovated and updated parts of it, I've also preserved certain elements that were quintessentially Estée, such as her collection of blue-and-white antique porcelain displayed on brackets in the living room, her blue-and-white ikat-stripe bedroom, and her glamorous formal dining room. I am also fortunate to have much of the crystal, china, and silver that she used in this home.

Furnished with her antique sideboard, Regency dining table, and Federal-style chairs, the dining room will always remind me of Estée. For special family dinners or formal dinner parties, I enjoy taking out her finest pieces, from the cut crystal candelabra and glasses to her silverware and chargers, because I know she would want them to be used. I've been collecting vintage and antique floral china, and it feels right at home in this room. I don't worry about finding complete sets because I love to mix and match. The custom tablecloth feels like an opulent garden, and I layered flowers here, from the centerpiece to the plates to the fabric. I believe sometimes more is more, and you shouldn't play it too safe, or it will feel boring. While I don't use as much pattern as my grandmother did (for example, I have monochromatic sisal and seagrass rugs rather than ornate carpets), I'm not afraid of color and pattern, and I find it makes any setting prettier, more inviting and distinctive.

I bought a pair of these pretty blue-and-white Chinese porcelain vases at the auction of the estate of Pierre Bergé, the partner of Yves Saint Laurent. They reminded me so much of my grandmother's collection and felt very appropriate for the house.

The gracious Georgian-
style architecture and
spacious entry offer a
welcoming arrival for
guests. I loved the plaster
chandelier in Estée's Palm
Beach house so much that
I had it copied to hang in
this entrance hall.
I've added woven sisal
matting that dresses
down the house for family
living at the beach.

Candlelight is magic. Dim the lighting and always light candles on the table for a dinner party, whether they're tapers, votives, or hurricanes. In this dining room, the chandelier is also candlelit, which creates a warm, intimate glow.

Even for a small dinner party, I like to add personal touches wherever I can. I had menu cards hand-lettered by master calligrapher Bernard Maisner to lend an old-world elegance befitting Estée's formality. Small footed bowls of silver-coated Jordan almonds are another very Estée touch. I kept the flowers all white, with a profusion of dahlias, roses, and cosmos that have a fresh-picked naturalism. Two potted gardenia trees flank the buffet, adding height, lush greenery, and wonderful fragrance. They create the feeling of being outdoors, while the white blossoms connect to those on the sideboard and the table. I found the elegant antique Waterford crystal chandelier in London. It is not electrified; it uses actual candles, so it casts an old-fashioned, romantic glow.

When the table is formally set, and we sit and eat in this room, I am connected to treasured memories and feel I am continuing traditions my grandmother established many decades ago, giving each meal a special resonance for me and my family.

OPPOSITE AND FOLLOWING PAGES: The dining room is a mix of old and new: Estée's candelabra, glasses, silver chargers, and flatware, along with my collection of vintage floral china, a flowering tablecloth, and bouquets of my favorite all-white flowers.

HOW TO SET A FORMAL TABLE

When you are setting the table for a dinner party, you should be guided first and foremost by what you are serving.

• I usually serve a first course, a main course, and dessert, so I set the table with two forks and two knives: one set for the appetizer or salad, and one set for the main course. (If your first course doesn't require a knife, or you're only serving a main course, then you won't need both forks and knives.) If you're serving soup, add the soup spoon to the right of the knife.

• Place the silverware in the order in which it will be used, from the outside in. So the small salad fork and appetizer knife should be placed on the outside, and the main course utensils next to the plate. The blades of the knives should be facing the plate.

• First course plates can be placed on the table atop the dinner plates, or served once everyone is seated. If you are using a separate salad or bread plate, that should be placed to the upper left of the dinner plate. Place the bread knife diagonally on the bread plate with the handle on the right and the blade facing down.

• I often layer a charger beneath the dinner plate. Remove the chargers when you serve the main course.

• I like to set the dessert spoon and fork above the dinner plate. The spoon should be placed on top, with the bowl facing to the left, and the fork below it, with the tines facing to the right.

• Glasses are placed to the upper right of the dinner plate, above the knives. The water glass should be on the inside and wineglasses on the outside.

• I fold the napkins (often in a triangle, but sometimes in a rectangle) and place them either atop the plate, or sometimes beneath the plate and hanging partway over the table. The napkin can also be placed to the left of the plate, either beneath the forks, or beside them. Always make sure your napkins are folded to display the monogram if they have one.

I like to set the table with two forks and knives, for the first and main courses, and then place the dessert fork and coffee or tea spoon above the place setting.
I often use chargers, like this silver one of Estée's, to set off the dinner plates.
I think in most situations, one wineglass and a water glass are sufficient.

Menu

Tomato soup

Roast Chicken

Potatoes

Purée peas

Chocolate soufflé

I feel very honored that Estée left me her collection of blue-and-white porcelain. It was an important source of inspiration for her, and so much a part of who she was. I enjoy living with it and adding my own updates to her iconic style.

There are certain elements in this house I've kept just as Estée had them, because I love them and they've had a profound influence on me—no doubt contributing to my own appreciation for blue-and-white patterns and beautiful porcelain—and also because they're talismans imbued with special memories. In the living room, I've kept the ornately carved and gilded brackets with her collection of Chinese porcelain vases, but I've pared back and updated the rest of the room with sisal matting, a white jacquard sofa, and a clean-lined blue lacquer Parsons table, giving Estée's more ornate antiques some room to breathe. There are certainly echoes of my grandmother in the blue-and-white throw pillows with branches and birds, motifs she loved.

I've also kept Estée's bedroom almost exactly the way she had it, but now we use it as a guest room. She covered the walls, windows, and furniture in Pierre Frey's Toile de Nantes ikat stripe, a pattern just as relevant today as when she decorated this room twenty years ago. That was Estée—she was both of her time and ahead of it, and she had the vision to tap into both current trends and timeless traditions.

In Estée's living room, I've pared back the patterns and formality, but I still love having her Chinese porcelain vases on carved brackets. While my sofa is all white, the pillows echo the vases. Our dog Biscuit is always my trusty companion, and the sisal rugs are a good choice for sandy feet and paws at the beach. Whenever I'm entertaining, I love to have fresh flowers throughout the rooms where guests will be.

I've kept my grandmother's tortoiseshell and silver-framed photos in the living room just as she had them, with pictures of us growing up and of her with famous friends including Princess Grace, the Duchess of Windsor, the Aga Khan, and Nancy Reagan.

With the exception of these Porthault bed linens and the straw rug, Estée's bedroom—which we now use as a guest room—is just the way she decorated it. She was the one person I've known who actually would have breakfast, tea, and sometimes even dinner in bed.

She loved to have breakfast in bed, on an elegant tray set with flowers, silver, and china. I think the only time I've ever eaten in bed is when I'm sick and have a cup of soup! But we could all take a page from her book. Before going out in the evening, she would often eat a small hamburger—also on a tray in her bedroom—so that she wouldn't be too hungry, or in case she didn't like what was being served. I can remember walking with my sister from my parents' house to visit my grandmother—she seemed to live such a glamorous life and would always indulge us with candy. She even had a little refrigerator in her sitting room filled with boxes of chocolates! Whenever I see a Godiva box, it takes me back to those special memories. I look forward to one day spoiling my grandchildren the way she spoiled us.

When Life
Gives You Lemons . . .

I had planned a beautiful end-of-summer dinner for twenty-four friends, journalists, and influencers to celebrate the launch of our newest fragrance, Limone di Sicilia. It was to be a lemon-accented Italian dinner with yellow tablecloths and bowls of fresh citrus in our backyard in East Hampton. Alas, the weather did not cooperate. The day of the party, it poured rain from morning till night. So I devised plan B. Instead of two long tables on the lawn, I rented two round tables and fit them in our dining room along with my round antique wood table. I used two similar floral tablecloths and left the wooden table uncovered, and it still looked feminine and charming.

With the change in color palette, we found pink dahlias and cosmos to better match the floral table linens. I mixed Estée's silverware, chargers, and crystal candlesticks with my Murano glassware and collection of vintage floral plates. It felt very significant for me to introduce my own fragrance in Estée's home. Just as she would have, I placed a small perfume bottle as a favor at each person's place, and we filled handwoven baskets with beauty products for everyone to take home. Sitting in Estée's dining room, enjoying a delicious Italian dinner, safely sheltered from the storm, I ended up thinking it was one of the most successful launch dinners I've hosted. Sometimes plan B turns out to be the best plan of all.

When rain threw a wrench in the plans for our Limone di Sicilia fragrance launch party, we quickly improvised three round tables in the dining room, instead of two long tables outdoors. I placed a bottle of our new perfume at each person's place, just as Estée liked to do.

Lauren Du Pont

THESE AND FOLLOWING PAGES: I covered two rented tables in similar floral tablecloths, and left my wood dining table bare, but united them all through striking pink dahlias, cosmos, and candles. The tables felt very cozy and inviting on a rainy evening. Crystal compotes filled with lemons on the sideboard carried through the original lemon theme.

A Celebration
of Friendship

So much of entertaining is about conjuring a mood—creating an ambience that blends a reassuring sense of warmth and welcome with a hint of excitement and a spark of wonder. The process is never entirely predictable—some nights turn out to be amazing, despite bad weather, kitchen disasters, or an important element forgotten. But on rare occasions, things just don't click, for no apparent reason at all. Careful planning and attention to detail will go a long way toward ensuring a successful and memorable evening. The single most important thing you can do is to put your guests at ease, focus on them, and be happily present, rather than running around stressed and overwhelmed and worried about what went wrong or isn't ready.

Sending a beautiful invitation, having a fragrant bouquet of flowers to greet guests when they walk in the door, along with a ready drink and bite to eat, the romantic glow of candles flickering at the table and in the powder room—all these are sensory cues that create a welcoming environment and sense of anticipation. I take into consideration all the senses when I am planning a party: the scents of flowers and candles; the background notes of music and conversation; the many visual pleasures, from the art and furnishings to the table; the silken touch of a tablecloth or velvety sofa; and the enticing tastes of the food, of course.

I was planning a birthday dinner for one of my closest girlfriends, and I wanted to make it perfect. I started with one of my most beloved sets of plates, by French interior de-signer Alberto Pinto. Called Histoires d'Orchidées, each one is a work of art, hand-painted with a different orchid on gilt-rimmed Limoges porcelain. The plates inspired the rich, luscious pinks of the flowers, an exuberant mix of ranunculus, anemones, and lisianthus, in hues shad-ing from pale pink to deepest violet.

OPPOSITE AND FOLLOWING PAGES: For a spring dinner, I wanted to play off the greens of the Fortuny curtains and tablecloth in my dining room with complementary pinks and purples in the flowers. The tonal bouquets of ranunculus, anemones, and lisianthus echoed the colors of the orchids in the Alberto Pinto plates. Hints of green are picked up in the candles and the Venetian goblets from Talmaris in Paris. Elements of silver, woven throughout the tabletop from the chargers to the candlesticks, helped tie it all together.

It's always nice when people leave a dinner party having met someone new. I like to include a guest who's just moved to the city or is visiting from out of town and seat them with people whom I think they would enjoy.

Those selections then led to another captivating element: the invitations and menu cards designed by Kinship Press. I actually discovered this wonderful bespoke stationery studio on Instagram, and met with Naomi and Alice Howarth, the talented sisters who hand-illustrate each unique creation, when I was last in London. Inspiration can come from so many places—travel, art, fashion, history—and Instagram has become a modern treasure trove of creativity from around the globe. I've discovered any number of little-known sources through my feed. I sent Alice and Naomi photos of my china, and the flowers I envisioned for the dinner and they created this illustration for the invitation and menu card that perfectly captures the stunning glory of the spring blossoms. The greens of the Fortuny tablecloth and Venetian glassware complement the pinks, and elegant accents of silver—my grandmother's chargers, and a vintage carafe and pitcher—are ideal companions to the gilded plates.

The final, very feminine pièce de résistance was the delectable, ruffled pavlova cake adorned with the same fresh flowers. I set up a dessert bar on the gilded console table with Estée's grandly scaled candelabra and some charming butterfly glasses and champagne flutes I found in Paris. And of course small bowls of sweets to finish the meal. This was one party where the inspiration and the image in my mind were matched by or even exceeded by the final result and, best of all, my friend said it was a birthday celebration she would never forget.

PREVIOUS PAGES: The vintage decanter in a silver coaster from James Robinson in New York was a wedding gift, and the napkins are from Leontine Linens in New Orleans.
OPPOSITE: Working with photos of my orchid plates and the flowers I planned to use for the dinner, Alice and Naomi Howarth of Kinship Press in London created a beautiful custom invitation and menu. We indulged in burrata with baby artichokes, lobster with spring vegetables, and refreshing sorbets.

I like to set up dessert on a sideboard or console when it's something special like this meringue cake from Lael Cakes in Brooklyn, so everyone can see it before it's sliced and served. Small bowls of candies and miniature fragrance bottles invite guests to help themselves. Estée's gold flatware, and fanciful butterfly and dragonfly glasses and champagne flutes I've collected, elevate the dessert course.

Please Come
Celebrate Spring

Dinner
at Home

Monday April 6
7:30 pm

INVITATIONS, MENUS & PLACE CARDS

Call me old-fashioned, but I still prefer to send printed invitations through the mail. They are beautiful, they set the tone for your event and create a sense of anticipation, and they're tangible reminders of the date as well as mementos to save, if you're so inclined. Of course, when I am just inviting friends over casually for dinner, I will simply text, e-mail, or call, sometimes spur of the moment or only a few days before. But for any special occasion party or formal dinner, I like to send a printed invitation.

• You can buy attractive preprinted invitations and fill them in by hand (or use your computer to print the event details), or you can order custom invitations through a stationer. For very special parties or dinners, I will sometimes go a step further and have invitations custom designed and illustrated. I've found a number of artists I enjoy working with to create something uniquely tailored to the event, including Happy Menocal and Kinship Press. Or I will enlist a talented calligrapher, such as Bernard Maisner, to create a hand-lettered invitation.

• For special dinners, I also like to have a coordinating menu card designed and printed. This carries the graphic style of the event through from invitation to dinner, adds an elegant touch to the table, and also lets guests know what will be served.

• At formal dinners for more than six or eight people, I prefer to use place cards. This eliminates that awkward moment when people aren't sure where to sit, and also allows me to think ahead of time about people who might enjoy meeting or talking to one another. Place cards are my secret ally in sparking the conversation and chemistry of the evening.

• Whenever I attend a special dinner or party at someone else's home, I think it is nice to send a handwritten note the next day or soon afterward thanking my hosts for the evening. I know they have put a lot of thought and effort into entertaining me, and I like to express my gratitude in writing.

The custom invitation by Kinship Press perfectly set the mood for the dinner. I always prefer to send printed invitations unless it's a casual or impromptu gathering.

A Whimsical Celebration
for Our Company

To celebrate the five-year anniversary of the launch of my company, AERIN, I wanted to host an informal but sophisticated luncheon at our offices. The occasion would honor my colleagues and their incredible hard work building the success of our brand. For any party, I look for that special element to spark the design or menu and take it to the next level, making each event feel memorable and unique. Whether I am hosting two people or twenty-two, it's all about paying attention to the details, thinking through each element to make it sparkle.

For this event, that element of wonder started with the dazzling creations of the Brooklyn Balloon Company. A friend had told me about their work and after viewing the inspired installations on their Instagram feed, I became obsessed. I reached out to see if they could design something for our office, and the moment of unexpected delight was set in motion. Balloons are typically thought of for children's birthday parties, but in Robert Moy's talented hands, these simple objects become works of art. In our airy white conference room, he fashioned a magical skyscape, stringing together balloons of varying sizes into a constellation of pastel colors, completely transforming the room. It was so mesmerizing we left them up for several days throughout our business meetings, because we couldn't bear to puncture the fantasy.

I love that our headquarters in the Fuller Building, an art deco gem on Fifty-Seventh Street in Manhattan, feels more like an elegant home than a dreary office, thanks to the exquisite furniture, modern art, and interior design mastery of Jacques Grange. The conference room, with its gold-leaf André Arbus credenza, 1950s mirrored table, Billy Baldwin étagères, and stunning Baugès chandelier, is no exception. For this workday luncheon just

In the entrance to our office, a cluster of balloons hints at the festivities to come. The Paul Lange photograph from his "Big Blooms" series sets a feminine tone for our fragrance and lifestyle company. FOLLOWING PAGES: The conference room was transformed for the celebration with an installation by the Brooklyn Balloon Company. Pink prevailed in single-blossom bouquets of dahlias, anemones, and ranunculus, and a rose-bedecked cake, pastel party ware, and candies.

Our brand is very much about surprise and
delight. The whimsical balloons and unexpected
mix of gilded objects and paper confetti,
penny candy and champagne, reflected that
element of fanciful wonder.

for our staff, we mixed lush flowers and tempting finger foods amid samples of our product designs and perfume bottles. Simple vases, each overflowing with a single variety of flower—exuberant dahlias, dramatic pink anemones, intricately ruffled ranunculus— echoed the feminine floral packaging of our fragrances, and roses adorned each tier of a gold-leaf-flecked cake by Magnolia Bakery. A dramatic but loose centerpiece of tall flowering branches grazed the chandelier. Our gilded porcelain flower objets, strewn across the table, carried through the theme. We served small bites that everyone likes, including heart-shaped mini pizzas, handmade potato chips, cookies, and of course, champagne. It was a festive, magical, and memorable celebration that transported us out of our everyday office routines, which was exactly the point.

THESE PAGES AND FOLLOWING: Look beyond typical decorations and don't be afraid to mix high and low: our gilded porcelain dahlias and daisy objets, paired with gold bowls, dressed up the table, while pastel paper confetti dots and starry Meri Meri paper plates lent an equally festive feel.

FLOWER ARRANGEMENTS FOR ENTERTAINING

Raúl Àvila is a remarkably talented floral and event designer in Manhattan whom I've known since my wedding. He and I have worked together for many years to create flower arrangements for our apartment in the city, for the office, and for brand shoots.

Here, Raúl shares his tips for arranging flowers for entertaining and suggestions for working with a florist:

• I always like to visit someone's home first when I am designing flowers for a party. From the moment I approach the house or building, to when I see the living and dining rooms, I am looking at the furnishings, fabrics, and artwork, the light in the space, the tablecloth and china they will be using—all of it. If they live out of town, then I want to see photos of everything. It's essential to consider the entire room and ambience when you are designing flowers. I take into account everything that will be on the table, because I want the flowers to blend, not to overpower the space.

• Particularly for Aerin—since she likes lush, monochromatic arrangements—but really for all the work I do, I want the flowers to look natural and have movement and dimension. I achieve this by cutting some stems longer, some shorter, using some flowers that are just buds, some that are starting to bloom, and others that are almost past peak, and I include the foliage as well. You want to see each individual flower and see them in different stages.

• It's important to condition flowers properly before you arrange them. A day or two before, we clean and cut the stems, place them in vitamin-treated water, and give them time to open up and settle. It's always best to choose flowers that are in season if possible. Flowers that have been forced in greenhouses are not going to look as good or last as long.

• Keep centerpieces low enough so that people can talk over them easily. To use a low bowl for an arrangement, add a ball of crumpled chicken wire or a block of Oasis floral foam and arrange flowers so they are cascading over the edge. Or use a series of smaller vases down the length of the table.

• To stretch your budget and to make the arrangement feel more lush, add lots of foliage. You can even create beautiful arrangements using foliage alone.

• In addition to a centerpiece on the dining table, place an arrangement in your front hall or wherever people will enter your home, to make a captivating first impression. Add a bouquet in your living room, maybe on the coffee table or other focal point. And it's always nice to have a small bouquet in your powder room. If you want to do something tall and dramatic, which you can't do on your dining table, the foyer or living room can be a good place, to draw the eye up and emphasize the height of the ceilings or a stunning chandelier.

• I prefer to use ceramic or metal vases rather than clear glass. Stems will soften and muddy the water, and detract from the appearance. There's so much attractive handmade pottery available, or make use of a beloved piece in your home.

• Don't be intimidated by arranging flowers. Even if you just place a few blossoms in a bud vase, it will be lovely because flowers themselves are beautiful.

The ombrélike pink anemones with deep purple-black centers don't need any embellishment to look stunning. Floral designer Raúl Àvila likes to include the flower's foliage for the most natural look.

A Luncheon
to Welcome Spring

While we spend the most time at our house in East Hampton in summer, we enjoy going out to the country in every season. It can be just as enjoyable to take long walks on the beach in early spring, or to cozy up by the fire on a fall weekend.

When I was about to introduce my tabletop line for AERIN, I wanted to invite friends over to see it and celebrate. To emphasize the early spring sunlight, and keep it somewhat informal, I chose to host a luncheon in our sunroom.

The starting point for the table was our classic creamware plates with a scalloped border, and hand-blown glassware from Murano. Particularly in spring and summer, I always like to layer in natural textures, like the abaca mats, straw vases and bamboo-handled flatware, which I actually use year-round. I find that adding chargers or woven place mats, even atop a tablecloth, beautifully frames and amplifies each place setting. When working with natural materials, everything mixes together effortlessly, just as it does in nature.

For flowers, I have been relying for years on Raúl Àvila, who is one of the most gifted floral designers I've worked with. He's the creative genius behind the elaborate, over-the-top floral fantasies at the Met Gala and many Paris couture shows, but he also creates simpler, equally enticing arrangements for entertaining at home. He intuitively understands by now what I love. That's the benefit of working with a particular florist or designer regularly—they soon know your taste and it's easier to communicate exactly the look you're envisioning.

Here, we decided to use all-white flowers with touches of greenery to complement the white tableware and the fresh beauty of spring's early buds. I prefer to work with an edited palette, focusing on varied tones of a single color, but spread across multiple vases—

Nature and natural textures always feel at home on the table:
a simple bowl of lemons, abaca place mats, and bamboo-handled
flatware are well-suited to the sunroom setting. A pair of citrus
trees makes it feel like we're eating out in the garden.

Creating a harmonious composition is often just intuitive, and only after I've finished arranging a table will I notice how the pierced, scalloped edging of our Paulette plates and centerpiece bowl is echoed in the open weave of the round wicker chair backs, circular straw vase holders, and abaca place mats.

Lacy majolica plates, left, and a fruit bowl, opposite, create an airy feel. Different textures and shades of white flowers bring richness and depth to a monochromatic composition, from the chartreuse-tinged buds of the lilacs to the delicate constellations of Queen Anne's lace.

usually one large centerpiece, with smaller satellite arrangements around it. This approach looks especially lush and abundant, and fills the entire table with flowers.

An equally important element in any event is the tablecloth. It helps set the palette, mood, and backdrop for the table. I love to find beautiful fabrics and have them made into tablecloths, a trick decorator Daniel Romualdez taught me. Particularly when I'm in the country, blue and white is a palette I often turn to—both because Estée loved it and used it throughout this house, and because it naturally evokes the sea and sky.

My mother taught me the easy, bright touch that a bowl of fresh fruit can add to the table. She is partial to green apples, but here I added vibrant yellow lemons for a punch of color that complements the blue and white. A bowl of lemons or cherries is something anyone can do in a second and it suits my casual style.

The result is a fresh and light table that captures the sunny optimism of spring.

The Comfort
of Kitchen Dining

For more casual lunches or dinners, I love the intimacy and relaxed feel of eating in the kitchen. Whether it's just neighbors or even a small dinner party, there's something so inviting and personal about welcoming guests into the heart of your home. I'm partial to all-white kitchens, and in the country I have creamy white cabinets and an island with caned white stools, as well as an informal dining area with a farmhouse table.

When we're hosting weekend guests or having family over, I like to set up breakfast buffet-style on the kitchen island so people can just help themselves whenever they wake up. I still want it to be pretty, so I put out my grandmother's silver tea service, pour orange juice into a decanter, add my hand-painted floral china teacups from Italy and linen napkins. And I always have flowers, of course, even if it's just simple wildflowers in a classic spongeware urn. This island is also where my sons once did homework with a snack at hand, and when it's just the four of us, we'll often eat lunch here.

In the eat-in area of our kitchen, a white-painted farmhouse table is surrounded by comfortably cushioned, pale wicker chairs I found in London, the same as those in my sunroom. The same elements I use to entertain there—raffia and straw, white earthenware and bamboo—adapt just as easily to the kitchen, but here I keep it simple with small, loose flower arrangements and no tablecloth. In fact, sometimes after I've hosted a dinner party and the house is filled with fresh flowers and looking its prettiest, I'll serve an informal lunch or brunch in here with leftovers the next day, to take full advantage of the setting.

Glass-fronted doors in our kitchen pantry make it easy for people to help themselves, and for me to see everything at a glance when I'm selecting pieces to set the table. Larger serving pieces are stored in the cabinets beneath. My collection of antique white ironstone pitchers creates a pleasing visual rhythm while also being functional.

Setting up a breakfast buffet lets guests serve themselves on their own timetable. Even with the informality of the kitchen island, I like to pour juice into carafes and to use my silver tea service, china teacups, and linen napkins. An antique spongeware ceramic urn given to me by my mother is perfect for holding wildflowers. FOLLOWING PAGES: For kitchen dining, no tablecloth needed. Our Italian heathered linen napkins add a splash of blue to a table of white and natural textures.

ON COLLECTING

For me, entertaining and collecting have a symbiotic relationship. Seeking out beautiful plates or unusual serving pieces can often lead you on the path to collecting, while setting an artful table can be a wonderful way to display and use your collections.

Collecting is a very personal passion, sometimes connected to value, history, or rarity, but more importantly to meaning, memory, and pleasure. It's all about embracing what you love and enjoying it. Some suggestions:

• Your collections do not have to be valuable; they only have to instill joy and have meaning to you. Sometimes they start quite spontaneously—when you realize you've accumulated more than four sets of salt and pepper shakers, or you've inherited your grandmother's willowware china, or you start picking up antique linens at flea markets. Whatever attracts your eye, pay attention to it.

• Look for meaningful additions to your collections on your travels, both to enhance your journey and conjure happy memories once you're home. I've bought napkin rings on safari in Tanzania, colorful candles in London, and plates in Panama. I often find inspiration through travel.

• Once you start a collection, learn about it. You will get greater enjoyment from your collecting and will make better, more informed purchases. You can learn by talking to knowledgeable dealers or shopkeepers, researching online or in books, or connecting with other collectors.

• Don't feel you have to find perfect matching sets. I love my collection of mismatched floral china in the Hamptons. The mix of floral patterns in similar colors, with touches of gilding, makes for a lively, individualistic table.

• Don't be afraid to use your collections. My mother, who collects very fine antique pottery and glassware, actually sets the table with it. If there are pieces that are especially valuable (even for sentimental reasons), consider displaying them on the wall—as Daniel Romualdez does with his seventeenth-century delft plates—or on plate racks, as my mother does in the Hamptons. That way you can enjoy them every time you pass through the room, not just when you're entertaining.

• By the same token, take good care of your collections. Store platters in cabinets with vertical tray dividers, or on secure plate racks. Place felt rounds or foam dividers between antique plates. Store silver in lined chests or bags made of anti-tarnish cloth. Fine crystal and glassware should be stored right side up, so as not to put pressure on delicate rims. Or invest in quilted, divided cases to store and protect infrequently used pieces.

My mother's collection of early American spongeware pitchers fills the open shelves in her living room in the Hamptons. Her very focused collection makes for a striking, graphic display that becomes a form of art.

SUMMER

I love to entertain in summer. The days are longer, foods are at their freshest and most delicious, people are more relaxed, and eating outside is enchanting. Nature creates a captivating backdrop, so it doesn't take much to set an inviting table. Flowers from the garden or a nearby farmers market can be arranged effortlessly into a vibrant centerpiece. It's easy to throw some steak or burgers on the grill, make a big salad, and mix up some sangria. Summer is also a time when it's fun to travel a little farther afield, whether to host a clambake on the beach or a picnic lunch on the water. And when my sons and their friends are here, we can always squeeze in a few more people on the picnic benches. Glass hurricanes with candlelight and the twinkling of fireflies, the scent of salt air or freshly mowed grass, and the sublime tastes of fresh corn and tomatoes, lobster, or a juicy burger are all it takes to have a good time, to appreciate the bounty of the season and the joy of good company.

A Poolside Lunch

We spend most of our time in the city, so coming out to the country, where we have a backyard in which to grow flowers, walk barefoot on the grass, swim in the pool, and entertain friends and family, is a true luxury. Of course, when you're going to host a party or meal outdoors, there always has to be an alternate plan in case of inclement weather, but most of the time the weather cooperates and it is wonderful to eat in the sunshine and fresh air.

On many summer Sundays we have a casual lunch of salads, cheeses, and rosé for any friends who are visiting, and we often invite my parents to join us. As always, even when it's just family, I like to take the time to set a pretty table.

I use a long, rectangular table with picnic benches, so the mood is casual and swimsuits and coverups are welcome. It's nice to place the table in a shady spot, so we had a pergola built that was inspired by the rustic, vine-covered dining arbor my mother created at their house. Ours is more classic and architectural, but it serves the same purpose, providing shade, a sense of shelter, and a defined space. This corner of the yard is surrounded by white hydrangeas, a picturesque backdrop for the table.

OPPOSITE AND FOLLOWING PAGES: A sunny yellow tablecloth made from Carolina Irving fabric, and natural textures like raffia, wicker, and bamboo set a summery table in the backyard. We created a shady spot for dining beneath a canopy of trees and a pergola overlooking the pool. Surrounded by hydrangeas, it's a lovely place for a meal any time of day or evening. I like to use a long table and benches outside for informality—it makes it easy to tuck in an extra guest or two when needed.

The best summer dining combines some of the niceties and comforts of indoors with the relaxed, easygoing attitude and freedom of eating outside.

A refreshing lemon-yellow tablecloth with white flowering vines creates an inviting oasis beneath the leafy trees. The raffia-wrapped glasses and vases add natural texture to the table. I filled the vases with a mix of unpretentious white daisies, zinnias, cosmos, and feathery astilbe, picked from our garden as well as from the farm stand up the road. Placing several small arrangements down the length of the table, rather than one large centerpiece, creates a casual yet pretty effect.

I discovered a wonderful small atelier in Milan, where a mother and her two daughters hand-paint china to your specifications, even personalizing it with an intricate monogram. The charming trumpet flowers, butterflies, painted borders, and elegant initials make these plates one of a kind. My favorite fluted Italian pitchers and swirled carafes are simple, summery accompaniments that let everyone serve themselves. Sitting here in the dappled sunlight, enjoying the company of family and friends, it's hard to imagine a lovelier spot for lunch than our own backyard.

This china was a special find when I was traveling in Italy: a mother-daughter team hand-painted the design and my monogram. Bamboo-handled flatware is a favorite choice in summer and a classic that isn't likely to go out of style.

Blue & White, Always Right

I think that a love of blue and white is encoded in my DNA. When Estée was first trying to decide on the packaging for her beauty products in 1946, she would go into friends' homes and ask to use their powder rooms, to see what color would look best there. She designed one of her first breakthrough products, Youth-Dew Eau de Parfum, in a robin's-egg blue bottle because she decided it would look good with almost any color of wallpaper. Her Hamptons home was (and still is) filled with her timeless collections of Chinese and Japanese blue-and-white porcelain and her bedroom is swathed floor to ceiling in a blue-and-white Pierre Frey ikat stripe. My mother has long collected antique American blue-and-white spongeware, and I have always been drawn to this classic color pairing as well. It is a perfect combination, particularly in summer.

There is no place I'd rather serve dinner than in our backyard in East Hampton. To eat outside by candlelight as the sun is setting and the fireflies start glowing is enchanting. With pitchers of sangria and platters of food fresh from the farm stand or off the grill, the cares of the city melt away and everyone can truly relax and enjoy themselves.

I set up a simple pergola made from iron and bamboo, which provides shade and a sense of shelter while letting light filter through. For a more formal dinner, instead of a long table with benches, I used my trademark round table with a tablecloth that creates the feeling of a blue-and-white bower. I chose understated white scalloped plates and napkins that don't compete with the detailed pattern of the tablecloth. Folding chairs are not expensive, and they're helpful to keep on hand for extra guests, indoors or out. My favorite summer textures of straw, wicker, and bamboo always seem to provide the perfect rustic counterpoint to blue-and-white patterns.

Blue and white are always an appealing complement to greenery. We chose this spot for outdoor dining because of its captivating view of the garden.
FOLLOWING PAGES: The natural textures of the bamboo pergola and chairs echo the trees, while the tablecloth evokes a blue-and-white garden.

Country blossoms like daisies, cosmos, dahlias, and freesia, all in white, pop against the blue, as do the rattan and raffia textures of the drink sleeves, place mats, and baskets.

94

I discovered these hand painted, leafy scalloped plates and teacups in Rome, made by Violante Guerrieri Gonzaga of Vio's Cooking (another wonderful Instagram find), and they instantly made me think of my backyard. Hand-embroidered blue forget-me-not napkins add a touch of feminine charm.

IN THE GARDEN

Entertaining doesn't have to be a dinner for twelve or even a luncheon for four. Why not invite a close friend over for tea on the patio or in the backyard one afternoon? Or even treat yourself? It doesn't take much effort to make teatime feel personal and special. My sons no longer use their tree house, but this shady corner of the yard is a lovely spot to pull out some rattan chairs and an ottoman from the pool house and set up a secluded place for entertaining. It's nice to change things up by taking advantage of different areas in your yard (or house) to enjoy coffee, a glass of wine, or lunch with a friend. It will give you a new perspective on your home. All it really takes is a tray to bring the accoutrements wherever you are, but a pretty tea set, linen napkins, and flowers will elevate even a casual get-together.

Seaside Accents

One of the pleasures of entertaining, for me, is the creative exercise of doing things a bit differently each time I host. While the room and background elements may remain the same, I am forever experimenting and varying the elements of the table setting to make it feel fresh. In our sunroom in East Hampton (seen dressed in blue and white on page 70), I hosted another luncheon later in summer. The pale wicker chairs, braided seagrass rug, orange trees, and some of my favorite wicker and raffia pieces were constants, but this time mementos of the sea and beach took the spotlight.

Though flowers are always lovely (and I usually include them in some way), consider thinking further afield for centerpiece ideas, whether it's a medley of candlesticks or a prized collection. I have been collecting pieces of coral on vacation for many years, and I love mixing its organic forms and intricate texture with the flowers on the table and the artwork on the sideboard. The texture of the coral is reflected in the shell-like whorls of dahlia petals and spikes of veronica, as well as the watery ripples on the glassware and hurricane candleholders. Antique Irish silver shell salt cellars and my grandmother's shell-pattern silverware give a nod to the marine ambience as well.

I chose a tablecloth in fresh green and white with leafy stems and blossoms to complement the flowers and greenery visible outdoors. The ropelike bullion fringe along its hem added to the nautical feel. Versatile wicker-wrapped hurricane glasses can be used for flowers or candlelight, and echo the woven raffia place mats and wicker chairs.

When you allow yourself enough time to enjoy the process and play with various elements, it can be very creatively fulfilling to compose a harmonious table.

It is my strong preference for tablecloths to extend to the floor. I feel it looks much more finished and elegant to cover the table legs and not have a cloth dangling halfway down. This green-and-white tablecloth is both fresh and luxe with its intricate pattern and bullion fringe grazing the floor. Bouquets of white summer blossoms with lots of green foliage are a perfect complement, while the large piece of coral connects to the seaside locale.

Rustic elements, like raffia vases and straw place mats mix unexpectedly well with fine silver. Special items like these shell-shaped salt cellars are great conversation pieces that add a personal touch to the table. Why not dust off family heirlooms or flea-market finds and actually use and enjoy them? Adding textured place mats atop a tablecloth frames each place setting, much like a charger.

FLOWERS & OUTDOOR ENTERTAINING

In the Hamptons, I've long relied on Michael Grim and Jim Osburn at the Bridgehampton Florist for flowers for our home and parties. They have an approachable, natural style and they know exactly what I like.

Here, Michael shares his pointers for arranging flowers and hosting outdoors:

• When I'm arranging flowers for my own home, I like to do them the day before the party, so they have time to fully open and relax, and also to lessen the stress on the day of the event.

• To gauge the proper height for a centerpiece, put your elbow on the table, and see where your wrist is; you don't want your arrangement to be any higher than that.

• If you're arranging flowers you've bought from the farm stand or store, give the stems a fresh cut, place them in the vase, then lift the whole bunch of flowers back up and give them a little shake to relax them and make them look more natural.

• For a long table, use several small arrangements down the table, rather than one large one in the center, so everyone can enjoy the flowers.

• If you'll be entertaining outdoors, don't take the flowers outside until close to the time of the party to keep them from wilting in the sun.

• When you create a centerpiece, think beyond just flowers. I like to walk through the house and find wonderful objects to add to the table, whether it's a piece of coral, a large shell, or a stack of books.

• If you're hosting a large group, instead of renting china, look at what you already own. It's fun to mix your grandmother's salad plates with modern white dinner plates to create a more eclectic feel. Don't give away old family pieces; find ways to use them with your existing collections.

• Candlelight is essential. It's nice to mix tall tapers or pillars with low votives. Use glass hurricanes outdoors to protect candles from the breeze.

• Always plan for the worst weather, then things can only get better. If you're planning to host twenty people outside, figure out how to make it work if you have to move inside.

• If it's a breezy evening, place napkins under the plate or the fork, to keep them from blowing away. And it's thoughtful to have extra wraps on hand for the women in case it gets cool.

• Some of my clients will plan two gatherings in one weekend to take advantage of the flower arrangements and having the house all ready.

Glass hurricanes or lanterns are a necessity outdoors to protect candles in the breeze, but they can be just as beautiful indoors. Flowers and candles should be considered in concert when planning the table. These tall, clear hurricanes add height without obstructing guests' views.

Elements of a successful still life: something from nature—a plant, coral, or shells; texture—here the coral adds tactile richness, as does the straw tray and woven table; varied heights; and a touch of color, like this antique botanical print in a whimsical frame, which underscores the natural theme.

Fourth of July on the Water

There are certain entertaining scenarios I have long pictured in my mind and sometimes I have the wonderful opportunity to make them come true. I had always envisioned hosting a casual but chic lunch aboard a boat in summer. Then I learned about this handsome, classic 1930s picnic boat, the *Mary Lloyd*, which could be rented near our home in the Hamptons. *Et voilà*, my seaside fantasy was realized.

For a picnic, whether on a boat, at the beach, or in a park, it's best to keep the food uncomplicated, but fun to make the meal unexpectedly elegant with real plates, linen napkins, silverware, and glasses rather than disposable plastic. For this lunch, a traditional wicker picnic basket helped set the tone, and even had cubbies for safely transporting wine bottles. Crisp picot-edge napkins with my monogram in the shape of a sailboat added a suitably nautical touch. Our raffia fish place mats, Murano glasses and pitcher, and scalloped plates further elevated the meal. Classic lobster rolls from one of our favorite spots, The Seafood Shop, are an easy yet indulgent treat appropriate to the seaside setting.

The result was such an enjoyable afternoon and a meal worthy of the striking setting. Take advantage of the opportunity to host a meal somewhere beautiful and unexpected any time you can. From a country field to a waterfront locale, the setting will instantly make the gathering memorable, requiring less effort and worry on your part about decorating and cooking (as long as the weather cooperates!). We couldn't have asked for a better day or spot to celebrate the Fourth of July!

OPPOSITE AND FOLLOWING PAGES: The place settings add a crisp nautical flavor, from the blue-striped Murano glasses and pitcher to fish-shaped straw place mats and sailboat-monogrammed linen napkins. I opted for white ceramic plates, but for unbreakable options, bamboo and melamine plates now come in many appealing patterns.

MARIA HUMMER-TUTTLE

"In reflecting on people whom I believe to be inspired hosts, I note a commonality of impressions: warm, thoughtful, gracious, authentic, enthusiastic, imaginative, attentive to detail. They are kind and they are fun. You are glad you came." —*Maria Hummer-Tuttle*

When I first met Maria, I was immediately drawn to her impeccable style, femininity, and grace. I met Maria through my parents. Her husband, Bob, was U.S. Ambassador to the United Kingdom; my father had served as U.S. Ambassador to Austria, and Maria, my mother, and I all serve on the board of the Foundation for Art and Preservation in Embassies (FAPE). Maria is an accomplished lawyer with exquisite taste who loves to entertain and collect antiques and handcrafted pieces in her travels, just as I do. Whenever Maria and I get together, we enjoy indulging our shared passion for entertaining and exchanging ideas, favorite stores, and off-the-beaten-path sources.

Maria and Bob live in Los Angeles, surrounded by roses and boxwood gardens, and she cuts and arranges her own flowers. "I generally create centerpieces from what we grow—whether it's roses, or lemons from our fruit trees, or just greenery," she says. In Southern California's climate, there are almost always some kind of roses in bloom in her garden, not to mention California poppies.

If her gardens are a perennial, abundant source for her centerpieces, Maria's frequent travels and love of collecting provide a palette from which to design her artful table settings. Her collections include antique silver, hand-painted

Maria Hummer-Tuttle gathers and arranges roses from her own garden in the foyer of her home in Los Angeles. The height and abundant foliage of her roses makes for a dramatic arrangement. FOLLOWING PAGES: Maria's elegant dining room is set for a baby shower and tea, with whimsical dolls interspersed among her elegant silver serving pieces, and an abundance of pink roses from her garden as the centerpiece.

porcelain, Venetian glass, and many finds that have captured her eye in Asia or in a Paris flea market. She is modest in discussing her favorites, but if you persist, each piece reveals a backstory. For example, she and Bob found the antique chandelier on their honeymoon in Paris, and it has moved with them from house to house over the years, whether hanging in an entrance hall or, as it does now, in their dining room. The unusual carved elephant and obelisk on a terra-cotta base in the loggia is a piece Maria fell in love with and bid on at an estate sale, but lost to another bidder. Some years later, "Bob discovered it in the window of an antiques store in Paris and surprised me with it for Christmas," she recalls. With such romantic tales woven into each element, their dinner table and home have become a history of their life and travels together.

There are some unique and whimsical pieces that are particular favorites of Maria's, such as an antique toast rack—a gift from a friend—which has a reservoir for oil with a wick to keep the toast warm in very old, cold, and drafty houses. Or the silver hippo that's actually a sugar bowl, with a bird sitting on top as its handle and his tail a small spoon. As Maria puts it, "To me it is fun to create a table, conjure a memory or an atmosphere that delights your guests. It is a form of self-expression and creativity on a small scale. To entertain is to bring people together, to share one's home and table, to celebrate life's milestones or simply honor friendship."

Having entertained in a formal way for her husband's ambassadorial role in England, but also over many years for both business and pleasure, Maria knows more than many people about how to host a successful dinner party. "I have a few self-imposed rules," she allows. "One is: it is dinner, not Noah's ark. I invite couples, of course, but also individuals, and seat guests according to perceptions of shared interests or chemistry, frequently defying the traditional man/woman seating." Her other piece of advice is both very simple and very wise: "Make it engaging for you and it will be engaging for others. Don't worry too much about rules, just enjoy."

A basket of fresh lemon branches clipped from fruit trees in Maria's yard creates an informal centerpiece for dinner on the loggia. The table can expand to seat as many as twelve. A white matelassé tablecloth is layered over a chartreuse skirt matching the napkins. The Alberto Pinto plates each feature different cabbages, befitting the garden setting, and the glassware is from Venice.

For a romantic dinner for two in the green garden, a small folding table
is set as elegantly as the finest restaurant's, with antique floral china
found at the Paris flea market, Venetian goblets, and ornate individual
silver casseroles. Maria likes to layer tablecloths for a luxurious effect.

Vegetable sushi, above, glistens like jewels, for an enticing appetizer. The cosmopolitan
table setting features intricate gilt-edged china and gold dessert spoons found
in Paris, mother-of-pearl flatware, and silver chargers that are family pieces. Maria has
collected the special silver bowls that look like small pumpkins over many years.

THESE AND PREVIOUS PAGES: The breakfast room overlooks the green garden, and is set for lunch with
a flowering Porthault tablecloth that echoes the freshly picked garden roses. Leafy hand-painted
Alberto Pinto porcelain plates rest atop glass plates Maria found at the Aurora restaurant on Capri.
Mouthwatering caramel soufflés, above, are served in silver ramekins from Provence.

London artist Luke Edward Hall's modern, whimsical take on antiquity and the sea features in his tableware for Richard Ginori, which Maria set on a table for two in the green garden. The silverware was her mother's; the pale pink of a single large hydrangea is echoed more deeply in the glassware.

The storied elephant obelisk Maria's husband purchased for her sits on the loggia table. The straw mats festooned with small shells and the beautifully embroidered coral napkins create a simple but sophisticated setting for lunch. Maria often picks fruits and flowers from the garden to decorate the table, including the apples and greenery seen here.

Maria gives guests the royal treatment with breakfast in bed. Two of her favorite pieces, a silver hippo sugar bowl, opposite, and an antique silver toast rack and warmer, a gift from a friend, add a unique touch.

FALL

Autumn is a season for returning to routines and catching up with friends. With a crisp chill in the air, everyone coming back from vacation, and the start of school, the city begins to hum again and I look forward to reconnecting with people. I turn to rich, deep shades of burgundy, loden green, and plum in flowers, tablecloths, and fashion. Dahlias are one of my favorite flowers, and at this time of year I use them to capture the brilliant shades of fall foliage on my table, from golden yellows and saffron orange to amber and crimson. It's a wonderful time to bundle up and go outside for a football game or hike, or cozy up inside by the fire. Entertaining at home, I tend to dress up more, add touches of gold to my table and interiors, and light more candles to combat the earlier nightfall. In many ways, this is the most picturesque time where I live, with the spectacle of changing leaves and skies. Fall is a season when my focus returns to home and the welcoming warmth of sitting around the table with friends old and new.

An Intimate Dinner
for Four

Sometimes a shift in the setting—from the predictability of the dining room to a less-expected or lesser-used part of your home—can spark a creative shift in your thinking. I love to entertain in every part of our home, from the library to the living room or even the kitchen or entryway.

In the foyer of our apartment, amid the modern art and mid-century French furniture, is the perhaps surprising addition of an eighteenth-century Beauvais tapestry hanging on one wall. Soon after we moved in, I found this tapestry and decided it would make a dramatic yet warm backdrop for the space. Perhaps it reminded me of my grandmother's opulent New York town house. When I placed a small round table in front of it, the woven scene created an enchanting tableau for an intimate dinner with friends. It also provided a rich palette from which to pull color cues for the table. A luxurious Fortuny fabric I had made into a tablecloth, paired with gilded 1920s French chairs by Armand-Albert Rateau, created the harmonious formal setting I had in mind. I set the table with some of my favorite silver, including a Revere bowl and mint julep cups filled with the deep, saturated shades of aubergine anemones and fuchsia ranunculus.

OPPOSITE AND FOLLOWING PAGES: Even for a small dinner for four, I enjoy setting the table with my best silver, from a vintage carafe and candlesticks to silver mint julep cups holding bouquets of ranunculus.

Sometimes, more is more. I love to add extra bouquets of flowers to the table and bring out my best silver and china. One of my favorite indulgences is having fresh flowers in the house even when I'm not entertaining.

To me, the pleasure and artistry of setting the table is found in considering every detail and blending unexpected elements. Where cut crystal goblets might seem de rigueur, I instead chose simple yet still refined green tumblers, and when I chanced upon the perfectly hued gray-green candles in London, I was crazy enough to hand-carry them back in my luggage. However, I also like to rely upon certain constants—like the silverware I registered for when I got married, from James Robinson in New York, and monogrammed white linen napkins, both of which I enlist regularly for formal place settings. There's no need to entirely reinvent the wheel: put effort into the elements that are most important to you, and streamline your decision-making by keeping other choices consistent.

This intimate, elegant setting instantly created a memorable evening.

The silver on the table gleams against the dark backdrop, including English candlesticks from Scully & Scully, my wedding silverware from James Robinson, and my grandmother's intricately detailed chargers. I found the green glass tumblers at Muriel Grateau in Paris and the perfect gray-green candles at Penny Morrison in London.

Come for Cocktails

One of the simplest ways to entertain is to have friends stop by for drinks. You don't need to cook, it can be impromptu or a planned prelude to heading out to dinner. I believe in having a bar, console table, or even just a tray always at the ready, set up with drinks and snacks such as nuts and chips in small gold or silver bowls. That way, even if someone drops by unexpectedly, it's easy to make them feel welcome.

The other reason I love to set up a bar is simply because the accessories and accoutrements are so elegant, in some ways reminiscent of a bygone era—from decanters, shakers, and glassware to match strikers and linen cocktail napkins. In my own line, we have shagreen trays and ice buckets, agate coasters, sleek bar tools and bottle stoppers, modern crystal carafes and tumblers, even cocktail picks and small footed nut bowls. On a sideboard or coffee table, a skyline of bottles and bar accessories creates a stylish still life mixed with glowing candles, a small vase of flowers, and artwork or framed photos. A tray will help neatly contain and organize the various elements, and can make it easy to move the party to another room.

In one corner of my New York living room, atop a distinctive French cabinet, I have classic monogrammed decanters from Asprey that a dear friend gave to each of my sons when they turned eighteen, a silver carafe, and new green Murano glass tumblers all quietly mingling with the fine art. A silver bowl holds nuts or my favorite homemade potato chips. Two vintage stacked crystal lamps flank the composition. For me, it's always about the mix of antique and modern, high and low, and sculptural forms and materials that makes for an engaging tableau.

OPPOSITE AND FOLLOWING PAGES: Setting up a bar in the living or dining room serves many purposes. It makes entertaining easier and keeps guests out of the kitchen; it instantly says "enjoy yourself," and the bottles, decanters, and glasses, organized on a tray, can create a beautiful still life. In my living room, decanters from Asprey, a Josef Hoffmann vase, and AERIN olive-green glasses create a rich tableau beneath modern masters' art, including a Cy Twombly work and a Picasso sketch.

HOW TO STOCK A BAR

I remember visiting São Schlumberger's town house in Paris for drinks with my parents when I was a little girl. She greeted us in a red ballgown and had put out little silver bowls filled with irresistible potato chips. It was all so divine and luxurious, it made a deep impression on me. I try to channel a bit of her hospitality by keeping a well-stocked bar and my own favorite potato chips from William Poll always at the ready.

• To stock your bar, either for a party or just to keep on hand, here are the basic types of liquor to consider, in addition to red and white wine, beer, and champagne:

Vodka	Bourbon
Gin	Rye
Rum	Vermouth (sweet
Tequila	and dry)
Scotch	Cognac/Brandy
Whiskey	Triple Sec

• Don't forget nonalcoholic drinks and mixers, including tonic, club soda or sparkling water, soft drinks, and orange and cranberry juices. Bitters are are also good to have, and you'll need lemons and limes.

• How to estimate the amount of wine and liquor you'll need for a party? It's a good idea to have more than you expect, because it won't go bad. A rule of thumb: for a cocktail party or dinner with only wine, estimate one bottle for every two guests, served every two hours. Or, calculate one drink per average drinker per hour; then increase that by 25 percent to be safe.

• A one-liter bottle of alcohol makes roughly twenty drinks. For mixers, allow about one liter of tonic, club soda, or juice for every three guests drinking liquor.

• To have enough ice, estimate about 1½ pounds of ice per person, which includes what you'll need for ice buckets or coolers. Outdoors in summer, plan on twice as much ice.

OPPOSITE AND FOLLOWING PAGES: A tray can help organize cocktail essentials, and also makes it easy to move drinks and snacks wherever guests are. Elegant materials such as shagreen, marble, leather, silver, or brass give a cohesive, sophisticated feel. I find that stemless glasses can work well for both cocktails and wine.

A pair of leafy, branchlike golden tables beside a damask chaise in our living room creates an inviting corner for coffee, tea, or a drink. Gilded cups and bowls elevate the experience, even when it's just for me.

TEA FOR ONE

Furnishing a corner of a room for reading; having tea, coffee, or a glass of wine; or indulging in a nap can help encourage taking a pause in our busy days. At one end of my living room, tucked in a corner next to the fireplace, a gold damask chaise with a pair of artful tables is just such a spot for me. The chaise is positioned so that I can gaze out the window and enjoy a cup of tea alone, or chat with a friend. It's lovely to curl up there with a book or stretch out for a quick nap by the fire. Now that I've created this place, passing through the room and seeing it tempts me to stop and slow down for a moment or two. Whether it involves an enveloping wing chair or a comfy chaise, design can be used to foster the things we enjoy and want to do more of. Honoring the moment with a gilded teacup, a bowl of fresh berries, and a vase of flowers enhances the sense of ritual and sacred time for oneself.

A Stylish & Spooky Birthday

Like many families, we treat birthdays as extra-special occasions. My grandfather was born on Christmas Eve, so we always celebrated it together as a family. My birthday still starts with my parents calling to sing me "Happy Birthday," no matter where they are in the world, and having cake for breakfast. I've loved continuing these traditions with my own children. My older son Jack's birthday is on July 7, so we often have a Fourth of July celebration for him. My younger son, Will, was born on November 1, so his birthday party is usually a Halloween celebration. What child doesn't like to celebrate a holiday devoted to candy?

Each year as October approaches, I start seeking out creative Halloween decorations, clever piñatas, and fun candies. It's nice to host intergenerational get-togethers with parents and children, grandparents and friends. In the city, our normally formal dining room is transformed into a spookily chic space with black bats and orange balloons with black streamers filling the ceiling. Halloween is a holiday that celebrates creativity, and the fact that it's primarily for children doesn't mean it can't also have touches of sophistication. The Day of the Dead (Día de Muertos), observed in Mexico at the same time, inspires elaborate decorations like *calaveras*, or sugar skulls, represented here

Sometimes all it takes is a big bunch of balloons to set a theme. These fun bat-shaped and bright orange balloons with their trailing streamers transformed our dining room in an instant. Using enough of them to almost cover the ceiling was key to making a big impact. They can also be weighted or taped to hover closer to child height. Since Will's birthday inspired our annual Halloween party, I had a shimmering orange satin tablecloth made for the occasion. (I confess that it never gets used the rest of the year!)

Clearly, I like to go all out for holidays. Bouquets of orange pompom dahlias and yellow and butterfly ranunculus help set the palette, while gold bowls filled with candy, creative cakes from Magnolia Bakery, and playful cat-shaped plates from Meri Meri add to the festive spirit. I like to mix high and low, with Murano glasses and gold flatware adding unexpected elegance.

Will's birthday and Halloween party are like a candy dream for the children. It's the perfect time of year to indulge the child in all of us with sweet treats and whimsical decorations.

in artful bottles. Autumnal bouquets of orange pompom dahlias and golden and butterfly ranunculus are eye candy for the grown-ups, while fancifully decorated cakes from Magnolia Bakery and golden bowls brimming with sweets are irresistible to children (and adults!). Whimsical decorations such as witchy surprise balls, skeleton straws, sequined masks, and black cat plates all add to the fun. I'm never afraid to fashion a high-low mix, with colorful Murano glasses and even Estée's ornate gold flatware, which suited the warm palette.

I love that Will's birthday gives me an excuse to go all-out for Halloween, but the truth is, there's no reason not to approach holidays with childlike enthusiasm, even as adults. The spirit of entertaining is all about embracing any opportunity to celebrate!

I enjoy searching out all the artful little details that help communicate a theme. There are so many good resources now online. These smiley skeleton straws from Meri Meri make Halloween feel friendly, not scary, for the littlest ones, while sequined masks scattered across the table add shimmering decoration—or may inspire a grown-up to join in the masquerade!

Tequila bottles, decorated like the sugar skulls or *calaveras* made for Día de Muertos celebrations in Mexico, add bold black-and-white graphic artistry to the table, as does the cobweb cake with three-dimensional spiders from Magnolia Bakery. Whimsical Halloween surprise balls from Meri Meri keep little ones occupied without sugar!

JO CAROLE LAUDER

"We didn't have a set pattern of dishes. We just started collecting things that all seemed to go together and that's what we use. We've collected pieces over the years, and because it's all the same eye, they all fit together." —*Jo Carole Lauder*

I developed much of my love of table settings—beautiful plates and glassware and serving pieces—from my mother, Jo Carole Lauder. She always takes the time to make a table inviting, even if it is just a weekday dinner. When my boys were young, my parents would have the children over for breakfast on the weekends. My mother would call to confirm that the boys were coming because she was setting a proper table for them. She and my father are passionate collectors, and their devotion to modern art (along with the art of many other periods) is not only reflected on the walls of their apartment, but it has also influenced the ceramics my mother collects.

"When we were first married," she recalls, "there was an antiques store called Price Glover on Fifty-Seventh Street. We were walking by it one day, and a small display window featured a Thomas Whieldon plate. Even though it was from the mid-1700s, it looked like the background of a contemporary painting from the 1960s or '70s. That's what drew us to those patterns. It was almost like a Brice Marden painting in miniature."

My mother also collects more traditional pieces such as English creamware, salt-glazed pottery, and antique glass, as well as English spatterware, which she uses in the country. She has long been focused on early American antiques, particularly

OPPOSITE AND FOLLOWING PAGES: My parents' dining room and town house are characterized by the dynamic tension between the bold, iconic contemporary art and more traditional antique furniture. My mother creatively bridges the two with her collections. The English step-glass decanter and colorful salt and pepper cellars look modern, but are, in fact, quite old. My mother's trademark bountiful bowl of green apples also has a modern simplicity with its brilliant color.

spongeware, glassware, and quilts.

In the city, my parents tend to entertain more formally, but my mother takes a fairly modern approach to the table. Though their dining table is a fine early American piece, she tends not to use a tablecloth, and her centerpiece is often a large bowl of green apples. The simplicity, strong color, and modernity of that approach helps connect the more traditional furniture and tableware to the bold presence of the modern art in the room. "I love green apples, because then there's always something alive on the table," says Jo Carole. "Even when we're not using the table, it's nice to have that color and life."

The dining table is a square, which can be expanded or contracted depending on the number of guests. If they are hosting a large group, they may use three round tables in the dining room to seat thirty or so guests. "But it's good to keep it to a small group if we can," says Jo Carole. "I love to entertain six or eight people, because then there's one conversation, and everyone feels a part of it. We all attend so many large events in New York for charities and such that I think people really enjoy a small dinner at home with friends."

My family's love of sweets and whimsy is evident in the chocolate dogs on the table. "We have a black goldendoodle whom we love, and these chocolates from Teuscher look just like him. He's very friendly and loves parties and meeting people." My mother confesses, "He lives in hopes of being fed, so he's always nearby at any lunch or dinner."

The dining table is a perfect square when the leaves are out; it is an early nineteenth-century mahogany accordion dining table from Philadelphia. The Queen Anne carved walnut chairs, from the mid-1700s, were also made in Philadelphia. The elegant candle chandelier is eighteenth-century English.

"My mother and mother-in-law always set a beautiful table, and I think you learn from that."
—*Jo Carole Lauder*

Creamy white Staffordshire salt-glazed stoneware plates and platters from the mid-1700s and English eighteenth- and nineteenth-century crystal glassware, pitchers, and decanters contrast with the brilliant pinks of the roses and greens of the apples.

162

ABOVE: Contemporary art and sculpture contrast with the antique sideboard and crystal candlesticks. OPPOSITE: Small chocolate dogs from Teuscher add a touch of whimsy to the table, in a nod to my parents' beloved golden-doodle. The Trifid silverware from James Robinson is a modern-looking pattern with roots in the seventeenth century, befitting the span of their collections.

"It's just nice to share a meal with friends and family. It's fun to make it as beautiful as possible, especially for a dinner with your children." —*Jo Carole Lauder*

In the country, my parents' dining room is an ode to their collection of English spatterware and American antiques. "We collect and use things that are more informal in the country," my mother notes. "Though spatterware often has birds and hearts and flowers, we've chosen the ones that are more contemporary looking, such as the red and blue bull's-eye pattern, which I love."

The spatterware she collects was made in Staffordshire, England, in the early 1800s. In this wood-paneled dining room, my mother lined one wall with shallow shelves to display her collection so that it feels like art. She sets the table with simple early American glassware and silverware, with spatterware pitchers and brass candlesticks fitted with tall, colorful tapers as an informal but lively centerpiece. The graceful twelve-arm, antique brass chandelier from around 1800 is also candlelit, with multihued candles that echo the colors of the pottery. "The candles create beautiful light in the room—it's very pretty and soft," explains Jo Carole. "I found them at Marston Luce, a wonderful little antiques store in Washington, DC. That's also where I found the antique French napkins, which happened to be embroidered with my initials,

My mother's collection of early nineteenth-century English spatterware is not only set on the table, but also displayed on shelves to form a stunning backdrop in their dining room in the Hamptons. Tall, colorful candles reflect the palette of the pottery and form a simple centerpiece with the spatterware pitcher and pieces of earthen-hued English Whieldon pottery.

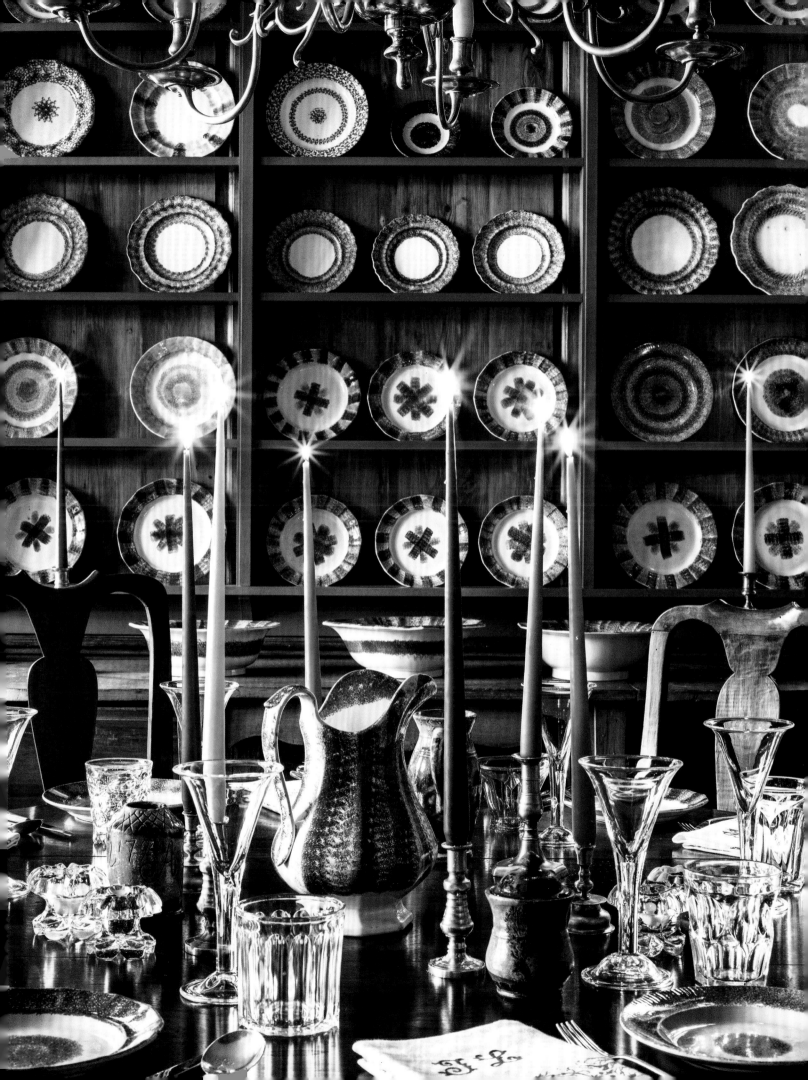

J.L." The early American furniture here is simpler than their antiques in the city, but the round table is a favorite of my mother's for entertaining, because it allows everyone to feel a part of the conversation.

"We like to entertain more informally in the country," she says. "We often eat outdoors on the porch or in a little trellised area in the summer, serving farm-fresh foods that are in season." My mother frequently uses her collection of Gmundner Keramik Austrian pottery (seen on page 192 in their rustic cabin), which she mixes with pieces from her blue-and-white American spongeware collection. The green- or red-and-white patterns of the Gmundner Keramik have a pared-back, graphic simplicity. "We lived in Vienna for two years, so I have a lot of the Austrian kitchen ceramics they make there. They look somewhat like the Vallauris ceramics that Picasso did," my mother observes.

While she often chooses not to use a tablecloth here, either, letting the pottery shine on its own, she sometimes will use early American quilts as tablecloths. My mother has more of a purist's approach to the table, reflecting her well-honed collecting instincts that have focused on particular types of ceramics and specific periods. I continue to learn from seeing how she puts it all together in a very clean, artistic, and appealing way.

The Queen Anne drop-leaf dining table and rush-seated chairs, made in Massachusetts in the mid-1700s, are simpler, early American versions of my parents' dining room furniture in the city. The dramatic, candlelit brass chandelier is early nineteenth-century Dutch or English. The polychrome pottery and candles brighten and enliven the wood-paneled room, which offers warmth and coziness for entertaining or family meals.

"I think what drew us to the spatterware were the shapes and the colors—they look like they could go with any period," my mother notes. A trio of pitchers on a side table, above, creates an artful still life.

DANIEL ROMUALDEZ

"When I entertain in the country, I prefer small, cozy dinners. I find it is the best way to catch up with good friends and get to know new people. Dinners in the country versus the city are more relaxed and leisurely, and can sometimes flow late into the night." —*Daniel Romualdez*

Daniel is not only an immensely talented interior designer and architect, he's also become a good friend. He decorated our house in Aspen and is designing a new vacation home we're building in Panama. He has an incredible sense of style, and I love visiting his country home in Connecticut. It's an eighteenth-century stone inn and farmhouse that once belonged to the iconic American fashion designer Bill Blass. To me, going to his house for a night is the ultimate sleepover. There's always a fire going, a delicious menu, dogs everywhere, and it's very luxurious but at the same time casual and comfortable.

"I like to set tables in all different rooms in this house," says Daniel. "It changes constantly based on the weather, from sitting outside at a small table in the garden to lingering over a fall lunch in the sunroom to dining by the fire in the wood-paneled sitting room on a cold winter evening."

One of the things I love about Daniel's style in the country is the masterful way he layers such an interesting mix of patterns, textiles, and antiques. "I collect plates and silverware, so I vary things depending

Architect and designer Daniel Romualdez, above, entertains more informally in the country than in the city. At his home in Connecticut, right, his collections of Dutch delft peacock china, on the wall and on the table, orchestrate a symphony in blue and white.

on what china I am using," he explains. "In the dining room, I've hung pieces of seventeenth-century Dutch delft peacock china that my friend Steven at Bardith found. The plates I use on the table are nineteenth-century versions, which are echoed in the tablecloth, made from an AERIN fabric for Lee Jofa. I tend to have fun with tablecloths because a fabric that might be too much in a whole room can be perfect on a table. And candles are essential in these rooms, which were most likely done in the eighteenth century, so they look best lit by candlelight."

Interestingly, Daniel isn't inclined to use floral centerpieces, with the exception of flowers from his garden. "I don't arrange the flowers—I just pick them from the garden and put them in a silver julep cup or vase. I use fruit just as often," he says. "I usually choose things that I already happen to have. I tend to focus on beautiful objects like quartz, coral, silver, and porcelain and I find that they can be well-suited to the table."

For Daniel, the food is the main event. "I love planning menus and I try to add things that are surprising, delicious, and homey. For instance, I'll serve a pasta sampler with *aglio e olio* and *vongole* on a balmy summer day, and on a frosty winter night, I love to serve variations on shepherd's pie or chicken potpie.

"While I like to keep things informal, I do have a structure, like planning who sits next to whom. Cocktail hour is short and I often make it obvious—hopefully in a polite way—when it's time for guests to leave, so I can catch a favorite TV show!"

For dining, Daniel uses nineteenth-century versions of the seventeenth-century Delft china displayed on the wall. A thrift-shop vase and a tablecloth made from AERIN for Lee Jofa fabric layer blue and creamy white patterns in varying scales. Antique shells on stands and horn-handled flatware add rustic contrast.

In the sitting room by the fire, Daniel sets a cozy table with wine, water, and vodka glasses (when indulging in caviar). A bowl of autumn fruit and a quartet of wooden candlesticks with glass hurricanes make a simple but inviting centerpiece. "The sofa in this room isn't too low and I sometimes use it as a banquette," he notes, which adds to the feeling of comfort.

Black-and-ivory florals and stripes set a crisp table in the sunroom. Daniel purchased the china and tureen from the auction of Bunny Mellon's estate. The wicker carafe, domed food cover, and water-glass sleeves and the vintage Buccellati bamboo flatware weave in natural texture. The tall, modern candle-sticks were a present from an Italian friend. Small, informal bouquets of white roses from the garden subtly echo Schumacher's Pyne Hollyhock fabric on the table.

WINTER

With winter comes the holidays and the most festive season of entertaining. Christmas, Hanukkah, and Kwanzaa make this a season of light, from garlanded Christmas trees to glowing candles. Everyone is in a frenetic but joyous state, rushing around to buy gifts and going to the many celebrations that all seem to be scheduled during the same two weeks in December. The holidays are a time when I love being with family and seeing old friends who are visiting from out of town, but I try to spread out the gatherings into January and February, when people have less on their calendars.

Come January, I confess that I often have a desire to hibernate, but I find I'm happier and enjoy the season more when I make the effort to entertain friends and get outside to ski or take walks in the snow. Even in the midst of winter, it's an inviting time to have people over for a drink by the fire or a hearty lunch in the country or to dress up for a glamorous dinner in the city.

Après Ski Dinner in Aspen

When we are fortunate enough to get away to the mountains of Colorado to ski, it's the winter version of "going to the country": everything is cozy, relaxed, centered on family and friends, being outdoors and being together. My husband, Eric, is an excellent skier and our sons have grown up loving to ski and snowboard. About ten years ago, we bought a modern house in Aspen that has a completely different feel from the classical architecture of our 1920s city apartment or Greek Revival country house. This contemporary ski lodge, with large expanses of windows looking out on the mountains, is furnished in all white, with lots of natural wood, Danish furniture, and modern ceramics. We feel surrounded by the majesty of nature from every vista.

Winter entertaining calls for hearty comfort foods like chili and hot chocolate, a rich color palette of browns and greens, and seasonal branches and blooms, like evergreens, red berries, and winter white flowers. Pine cones and even river rocks might become part of my centerpiece. My dinners tend to be small, casual, and likely to include just close friends and family. We might invite friends over for an après-ski drink by the fire or cocoa outdoors on the deck, cuddled up in throws.

We occasionally spend Christmas in Aspen, and there is no place more wondrous to be—you are guaranteed a white Christmas! I like to decorate a tree outdoors as well as in, so that from the dining table we can look out and see a glowing, snow-frosted tree trimmed in pine cones and touches of red and gold.

Over one holiday vacation we invited family friends to join us for a cozy dinner of chicken potpie. I often include the children and different generations when we entertain, whether it's grandparents or visiting houseguests. It's taught our sons to be both good hosts and guests, and the conversation is lively and interesting with different ages joining in. In Aspen, we have a long, rectangular table, rather than a round one, but I still like to dress it in a patterned fabric tablecloth. Green glassware and a modern version of brown

A large, vintage wooden tray can create an impromptu bar wherever it's placed. I will confess to sometimes choosing liquor bottles for their beautiful designs, like this bottle of Dalmore whiskey with a silver stag's head (thankfully it's a fine whiskey as well). Rustic dishes of nuts, a compact bouquet of berries, black-and-white gingham cocktail napkins, and a shagreen match striker add layers that feel warm and inviting.

In our large, open living room, the dining table sits opposite the fireplace and seating area, which is a cozy spot to have cocktails or after-dinner coffee. The white sofa, Hans Wegner hoop chairs that recall snowshoes, and a George Nakashima table are serene, natural pieces that complement the showstopping views.

spatterware pair with woven straw place mats, natural linen napkins, and wood-handled silverware for a table that mixes rustic with refined.

In the mountains I don't have access to as many kinds of flowers, but small bouquets of some of my favorite white blooms such as anemones echo the snowy landscape outside the windows. After dinner we gather by the fire for a nightcap, or sometimes even bundle up and sit outside on the deck to marvel at the stars. One can't help but be moved by the close connection to the outdoors here and the stunning natural beauty.

The more time outdoors here, the better, whether it's time spent skiing or sipping hot toddies on the deck. OPPOSITE: Spatterware plates and green cut-glass goblets from March, in San Francisco, are layered with natural textures like chunky woven straw mats and rustic wood-handled flatware. A potpie with a heart-embellished crust is the perfect winter supper. The naturally decorated Christmas tree, visible from the table, carries the holiday spirit outdoors.

The deck is the perfect place to be on a sunny day, sitting in comfortable modern teak chairs with views of Ajax Mountain, and hot chocolate and fur throws to warm us. Handmade marshmallows add a delicious finishing touch to cocoa.

189

Rustic Family Gatherings

We usually celebrate Thanksgiving with a traditional dinner at my parents' house in the Hamptons. The day after Thanksgiving, my parents host a casual lunch with turkey leftovers in an old log cabin on their property, which was originally a summer kitchen from Virginia. It is furnished with primitive Austrian wood furniture and filled with charm and history that transports us back to another era. We build a big fire in the fireplace, and have hot apple cider and apple doughnuts. I found charming red folkloric plates and bowls I thought would be just right for the cottage (or our house in Aspen) at La Tuile à Loup, a unique store in Paris filled with handmade pottery from artisans all over France. Red-and-white mono-grammed gingham napkins and horn-handled flatware provided the perfect accompani-ments. Terra-cotta pots of geraniums and vases of dahlias added splashes of bright red to the weathered wood.

My mother has long collected a type of hand-painted earthenware pottery made in Austria called Gmundner Keramik. These ceramics have been made in the town of Gmundnen, on the shores of Lake Traunsee, since the late 1400s. The whimsical green-and-white striped and looped Dizzy pattern, as well as the leaping Gmundner green deer, are some of my mother's favorite pottery to use in the country, and were just the thing for some cocoa on a chilly November day.

After the elaborate Thanksgiving feast, this simple, bucolic meal is the ideal anti-dote and it has become a beloved family ritual.

Simple pleasures are celebrated in this centuries-old log cabin on my parents' property in the Hamptons: bright red geraniums and dahlias pop against the well-aged wood of an antique sled table and the primitive Tyrolean chairs with hand-carved backs from Austria. Red-and-white patterned folkloric plates and bowls found in France, charming gingham napkins, simple glassware, and horn-handled flatware complement the rustic setting. A grapevine heart on the wall echoes the cutout motifs on the farmhouse chairs.

My mother started collecting Gmundner Keramik, folk-art ceramics made in
Austria, when we lived there. The simple, hand-painted stripes, loops,
and leaping stags are well-suited to the country. When I found these napkins
embroidered with deer, I knew they would be perfect with this pottery.

It can be just as creative—if not more so—to entertain in a rustic, bare-bones space as an elegant, luxurious one. The barn and cabin on my parents' property are two such unexpected settings.

My parents have collected and preserved a number of early American structures on their Hamptons property, including the cabin seen on the previous pages, and this lofty antique barn. For a holiday lunch, I hosted a small group of family friends in the barn, decorating it with fragrant fresh evergreens and pine cones. I had the sepia-and-cream tablecloth made from one of my fabrics for Lee Jofa. It forms a graphic backdrop for wooden chargers and wood-handled flatware, creamy stoneware plates, and gilded bowls filled with pears. The pièce de résistance was the dramatic, two-tiered iron candle chandelier crowning the table, woven with pine cone and pine garlands for rustic grandeur. Sprigs of pine and small pine cones were carried through as accents atop the natural linen napkins at each place setting. Big buckets of seasonal greens, black metal lanterns, and a centerpiece of green hydrangeas brought color and light to the simple setting. We dressed warmly and enjoyed a lunch of soup, cheeses, and sandwiches on home-made bread to celebrate the season in an unconventional setting filled with charm.

I recommend thinking vertically when decorating a dining area, particularly at the holidays. In my parents' barn, a large-scale iron candle chandelier festooned with evergreen and pine cone garlands crowns the table and creates drama.

Holiday Celebrations

Christmas in New York is a truly magical time. The city is dressed in its finest, with twinkling lights and magnificent trees, store windows filled with captivating displays, and an abundance of greenery, flowers, and the transporting scent of pine.

In my family growing up and now with my own family, we have always celebrated both Hanukkah and Christmas. On Christmas morning, my father would make us apple pancakes and we would open gifts in our pajamas, traditions I've continued with my own children. We observed the Jewish holidays at my grandmother's, and still gather there to eat in her stately town house, using her beautiful china and surrounded by memories. Sometimes we go to my parents' or my uncle's, but somehow the matzo ball soup always tastes best at my grandmother's.

December is an enchanting time to entertain and welcome friends to sit by the fire: the house is filled with festive bouquets of red flowers and fragrant evergreen garlands and the tree is glistening and adorned with ornaments. I have been collecting ornaments on my travels for years and giving special ones to my children, so trimming the tree is a nostalgic journey that offers us a chance to reminisce and recall all the places we've been together.

Christmas morning we gather by a cozy fire in the library and exchange gifts, listening to holiday music. The library is lined with classic red leather photo albums from Asprey that my mother carefully and thoughtfully creates for us each year, and hanging on the bookshelves are fine art drawings my father has given to my sons over the years. I still order an elaborate gingerbread house from William Poll, and even though my children are now grown, it always gets eaten. I make pancakes just like my father did, and we've been known to sneak a few bites of gingerbread and chocolate at breakfast. Those are the indulgences of the season, and we all love to partake in them.

We often put up our Christmas tree in the library, so that's where we gather on Christmas morning to exchange gifts, and it's also a cozy spot to entertain by the fire throughout the holiday season.

This room encapsulates everything I love about
the holidays, and it's where everyone gravi-
tates in December. Evergreen garlands adorn
the mantel, and the tree is lavished tip to trunk
with twinkling lights and meaningful ornaments
I've collected over the years. Festive bouquets
of butterfly ranunculus and purple anemones
and bowls of ornaments spread cheer to every
corner. The greenery, tree lights, and sparks of
red pop against the deep slate-blue walls.

The silver tea set was a wedding gift from my parents. Bowls of ornaments and colorful Christmas ribbon candy add a festive touch to the art books I always have on the coffee table. I still hang appliquéd Christmas stockings filled with small treats for our sons. FOLLOWING PAGES: Enjoying a gingerbread house from William Poll, and receiving a beautiful red leather album from Asprey filled with family photos—a treasured gift from my mother—are traditions we look forward to each year.

CAROLINE SIEBER
VON WESTENHOLZ

"We love to entertain at home, even with two young children. It's nice to have a lively and busy house. It is also the best excuse to buy place settings and table-top accessories, probably my favorite thing to shop for."
—*Caroline Sieber von Westenholz*

I met Caroline Sieber in high school in Vienna, where we were living while my father served as U.S. Ambassador to Austria. Even then, Caroline had a distinctive, confident sense of style. I reconnected with her in recent years thanks to Instagram, where I always look forward to her posts, which showcase her intrepid travels and incredible fashion sense. Her wedding to Fritz von Westenholz in Vienna in 2013 was spectacular and the images are worth seeking out for their glamour and artistry.

Christmas dinner at Caroline's London town house features some of their favorite treats from Demel in Vienna. Caroline is dressed in an Austrian dirndl–inspired dress by Karl Lagerfeld for Chanel, and her daughters Electra, three, and Cleopatra, two (and their maltipoo, Swifty) are all well-behaved enough to sit at the formal table.

Santa Claus and angel cookies from Vienna and Christmas crackers decorate each place setting. The silver Augsburg beakers, chargers, and vase set the table aglow. The Porthault table linens complement the Herend china. A romantic flower arrangement from Scarlet & Violet takes an updated approach to the holiday palette.

Caroline and Fritz now reside in London with their two adorable daughters, Electra, age three, and Cleopatra, two. They live in a stately 1860s town house next to Kensington Gardens, and Caroline has decorated it with her signature femininity, eclecticism, and whimsy. Whenever I am in London, I love to see Caroline and learn what she's been up to. As a fashion consultant she has her finger on the pulse of what is fresh and exciting but, as her home attests, she is also very much connected to the traditions and heritage of both her family and her husband's. It's that twist on tradition I can relate to, even if we express it in different ways.

Caroline shared an intimate peek at their family Christmas celebrations and traditions. "Right now," she notes, "our dining room is being redone, so we had our traditional Christmas dinner in the breakfast room. It's furnished more informally with wicker furniture I had made in Italy, near my parents' summer home. We use a lot of it around the house and it is painted in a custom shade of green that I adore." The distinctive, large-scale pendant lamp in a bright, graphic linen offers a modern counterpoint to the delicate floral-striped furniture cushions.

"My parents were quite old-fashioned," says Caroline. "Here in London I try to keep our home more relaxed and informal, though there are aspects I am keen to hold on to. At home in Austria, breakfast, lunch, and dinner were always carefully laid out. As children we used grown-up plates and cutlery, and we ate with my parents from as early as I can remember. We now do the same with our girls. It's important to me that they grow up with that sensibility.

"Our main Christmas celebration," Caroline explains, "takes place December 24, when the *Christkind* (Christmas angel) comes bearing gifts. The morning is spent baking cookies and wrapping presents. We then celebrate Christmas Eve in black tie. My husband grew up with the English tradition of stockings, so we have those on Christmas morning.

"The dinner table for Christmas Eve is set with our Herend Victoria china, which I love, and I chose the Porthault table linens to complement it. We have our favorite Christmas biscuits, cakes, gingerbread, and chocolates sent every year from Demel in Vienna." The whimsically decorated cookies and treat-filled Christmas crackers

In the drawing room, the pale green-and-ivory palette is reflected in Caroline's leaf-wreathed Herend china and table linens from her mother, and in the fresh and feminine bouquet by Vic Brotherson of Scarlet & Violet. *Meringata* (meringue cake) is the children's favorite.

serve as favors at each place setting. Ornate silver Augsburger beakers and other pieces of family silver set the table with tradition. The flowers were designed by Vic Brotherson of Scarlet & Violet, who has been doing Caroline's flowers for the past ten years, so Vic knows the house and Caroline's taste well. "For a particular party or table setting, I will send Vic pictures of the dinner service and linens," she notes.

The drawing room is set for a holiday brunch with close friends. The menu features classic Austrian pastries such as *guglhopf* (a traditional bundt cake) and *meringata* (meringue cake), the children's favorite. Savory dishes such as cold meats, smoked salmon, and eggs are also served. The green leaf-patterned china is from Herend, which is echoed in the Swiss table linens given to Caroline by her late mother. Even their beloved maltipoo, Swifty, is allowed to sit near the table, though she would never dare go near the food. Lavish white flowers and greenery complement the table settings perfectly.

As for entertaining wisdom, Caroline says, "Placement, of course, is crucial, and I prefer uncomplicated menus, and no music during dinner. Simple table settings are more elegant than ones that are overthought and overdone." Most importantly, "Have fun at your own party!"

Leaves of green in every form entwine the table: decorating the Christmas crackers, encircling the chocolate-box favors from Demel, adorning the china and table linens, and adding lush natural texture to the flower arrangement. In addition to the Viennese cakes and pastries, smoked salmon, cold meats, and eggs are served for brunch, so elegant silver salt and pepper cellars crown each place setting.

Christmas Eve Dinner

My grandfather was born on December 24, so we celebrated his birthday as a family—either at home or with dinner at the 21 Club   eating goose and chicken hash, with the Salvation Army singing carols and gentlemen in black tie. It's very old-school New York. Now I will often gather family at our home on the twenty-fourth and serve a classic English Christmas dinner with roast beef, Yorkshire pudding, and my father's favorite holiday dessert, a chocolate bûche de Noël.

For Christmas dinner, I like to refine the palette to red and gold for a festive approach to the season. Gleaming gold vases, bowls, candlesticks and hurricane glasses of varying heights provide a warm foil for vibrant red roses, peonies, and berries. Bowls brimming with candies and ornaments and small wrapped presents at each place setting remind me of my grandmother. I tend to use simple gold plates or chargers, but sometimes I will go all out and use Estée's opulent red-and-gold Russian dinnerware on a red-and-white patterned tablecloth. It's over-the-top and very festive and elegant. If there's ever a time to go a little overboard with decorating, it's at Christmastime.

OPPOSITE AND FOLLOWING PAGES: My dining room in the city, decorated for two different Christmases—one when the walls were a deep aubergine, with a green Fortuny tablecloth. On the overleaf is a more recent holiday, now that the dining room has lighter ivory walls, with a gold tablecloth. Though the backdrop might change, my preferences are revealed in certain constants, like multiple arrangements of vibrant red flowers such as roses, tulips, and anemones in gleaming gold vases, as well as gold chargers and stemless glasses.

HOSTESS GIFTS & FAVORS

My grandmother Estée was a brilliant gift-giver. She invented the gift-with-purchase concept in the cosmetics business because, as she pointed out, even the Duchess of Windsor enjoys getting an unexpected gift. At her dinner parties, she would place small perfume bottles or pretty compacts at each woman's place. She knew how to add those special little touches that make a party memorable.

• I like to continue my grandmother's tradition, especially at luncheons or dinners for girl-friends, adding a small fragrance bottle or scented candle at each place. I've also given favors like marble acorns or bud vases that can enhance the table settings or serve as place card holders.

• At the holidays, I make sure each young person has a little gift at the table, whether it's a beautifully iced cookie or a box of candies. I might wrap small presents or add Christmas crackers to make the table feel festive and keep the children entertained.

• When it comes to hostess gifts, I love to give one of our scented candles. Or I'll send a vase with a small bouquet of flowers (for a powder room or bedroom) the morning of the party with a note saying, "Looking forward to tonight." It's also a nice gesture to send flowers afterward with a thank-you note.

• I like to give the hostess gifts that I enjoy receiving. I love when people give me a book they've enjoyed, or chocolates or flowers. Even though people say not to arrive at a dinner party with flowers, because then the host has to worry about finding a vase and cutting them, I appreciate anything that someone makes the effort to bring.

• If I'm visiting someone for an overnight or the weekend, I try to give something a little more special. If you're traveling out of town, it's thoughtful to bring (or send ahead) some food specialties or delicacies from your own city. As a chocolate lover, I might bring a beautiful box of sweets from one of my favorite stores, like Teuscher in New York City.

Estée's ornate red-and-gold Russian china creates an opulent table in a holiday palette. Small brass bowls filled with red and green candies add a merry touch on the table and the bar.

The monogrammed double old-fashioned glasses belonged to my grandfather (they have both his and Estée's initials). I love embracing the tradition and heritage of my grandparents' home.

DRINKS IN THE STUDY

When my grandmother lived in this house in East Hampton, this rather small room, now my husband's study, was her kitchen. Needless to say, she did not spend a lot of time there. After I inherited her home, we waited a couple of years to make any changes, but we eventually added a larger, more modern and welcoming eat-in kitchen, which became the hub of our young family's life in the country. To reinvent this as my husband's study—a cozy refuge on fall and winter evenings—I painted the walls and bookshelves a dark blue-black, re-covered Estée's chairs in black linen, and added a tiger-patterned carpet and black lacquer

coffee table. This is a snug, inviting place to have drinks, just the two of us, or after-dinner coffee and whiskey with friends.

Gilded glasses, a good bottle of scotch, and a bowl of cheese straws, nestled among art books, linen cocktail napkins (always preferable to paper), and a striking vase of purple allium are all it takes to turn a simple table into an invitation to sit and enjoy a conversation. As much as I love light, it's also important to have the contrast of dark rooms as well; it creates intimacy and drama. Many bars or cocktail lounges are dark for this reason, so why not create that kind of cozy hideaway in a corner of your own home?

THE NEW GARDEN PARADISE

PHOTOGRAPHS BY KELLY KLEIN

ALLURE · DIANA VREELAND

ALLURE · DIANA VREELAND

OBAN

GRANDE RES

PLANTATION
RUM
BARBADOS

HIROSHI SUGIMOTO

Ringing in the New Year

For many people, New Year's Eve is an occasion to go out on the town, but it's actually a night when I prefer to avoid the crowds and chaos of New York City and stay in. While we usually escape to Palm Beach for the holidays, when we're in the city, I like to invite a small circle of friends for an elegant dinner at home.

For my New Year's table, I kept the palette to gold, silver, and white to create a look that's quietly opulent. I think gold works well as a neutral, which is why I have gilded chairs in our dining room and touches of gold throughout the apartment. My dining room used to be painted a deep aubergine, as a bookend to the slate-blue library visible across the living room, but I realized I preferred this room to be a lighter shade. A clean, neutral canvas gives me much wider latitude to change the table settings, flowers, and palette as I please for entertaining. The waterfall Ruhlmann chandelier strikes a glamorous note, echoed by the Fortuny curtains that frame the tall casement windows like lustrous ball gowns. For dinner parties, I'm partial to a round table, which—as my mother taught me—facilitates conversation and the feeling that everyone is at the same party together, rather than separated at opposite ends of the table. I chose a gold Fortuny fabric to drape the table and create a refined backdrop.

Estée's ornate repoussée silver wine cooler elevated the champagne to become part of the centerpiece, and I set the rest of the table almost entirely in silver as well, from the gleaming chargers and candlesticks to salt cellars and mint julep cups filled with all-white bouquets. For my wedding, I gave each of my bridesmaids a silver julep cup engraved with her initials and the wedding date. One can never have too many julep cups: they are perfect for small flower arrangements in a powder room or on a bedside table, and I also use them on my desk, in my dressing room, and for serving drinks, of course. The silver keeps them refreshingly cold.

OPPOSITE AND FOLLOWING PAGES: Gold, silver, and white form a classic, elegant palette for a New Year's Eve dinner. A mix of ornate antique silver pieces and vintage champagne flutes contrast with simple, modern Austrian wine and water glasses from the Neue Galerie. Similarly, this clean-lined, understated Oscar de la Renta gown is a canvas for the intricate craftsmanship of a butterfly necklace from David Webb.

Oversize Christmas crackers tied with lavish satin bows were created by Fiona Leahy. Large enough to hold small perfume bottles and other goodies as well as candies, they make charming favors for guests and add a festive touch to each place setting.

New Year's Eve called for some special, elevated touches. One was the hand-lettered menus by artist and calligrapher Bernard Maisner. His graceful script strikes just the right balance between old-world formality and modern simplicity. Another festive gesture was the oversize Christmas crackers created by Fiona Leahy, a talented event designer in London whom we've used to help with fragrance launches and press events.

I love white flowers: they are versatile enough to use year-round, and I think they're particularly elegant in winter. An abundance of simple freesia, with its creamy blossoms, plentiful green buds, and sweet fragrance, formed the centerpiece, while clusters of winter hellebores, peonies, and anemones filled each julep cup with a variety of textures and gradations of white.

As the evening stretched toward midnight and we toasted to one another's good health and happiness, I was once again reminded there is no better place to usher in the new year than at home.

Menu

smoked salmon

SEATING, PACING & OTHER HOSTING SECRETS

After hosting many parties and dinners over the years, I've developed some rules of thumb for a successful event. Everyone likes to entertain a bit differently, so there are no hard-and-fast directives; this just reflects what has worked best for me.

• For a dinner party, allow about forty-five minutes for cocktails before dinner is served. This gives people time to arrive and have a drink before the meal, but doesn't drag on so long that people get hungry or have too much to drink. It's usually just the right amount of time before moving on to the main event.

• Similarly, don't overdo it on hors d'oeuvres before dinner. I like to have some bowls of nuts and homemade potato chips, and maybe a couple small hors d'oeuvres that everyone enjoys, such as pigs in a blanket, but too much will ruin everyone's appetite for dinner.

• Never try to do everything the day of the party. I prefer to set the table and do the flowers a day ahead of time, so the day of is calm and not chaotic. Try to allow an hour ahead of your party to sit down, relax, and recharge to get ready for the evening.

• For a large dinner or party, if you can afford to hire someone to help with serving drinks and dinner and then cleanup, it will go a long way toward letting you enjoy your own party and serving your guests in a timely manner.

• I tend to invite a mix of people, some of whom know each other and a few new faces, such as friends who are visiting from out of town or someone I've met through work. I think it makes for a more interesting evening to include a blend of generations and backgrounds.

• When I'm planning the table seating, I split up couples, alternate men and women, and try to pair people who already know each other with someone new. Part of being a good guest is making the effort to get to know the newcomers and draw them into the conversation.

• After dinner, I like to serve coffee and tea in the living room or library. That offers guests a chance to slip out and leave if they need to, and it makes a smooth transition to start winding down the evening. Not that it always works: sometimes everyone's having a great time and the party just continues, and that can be wonderful, too!

A menu card—whether personally handwritten, lettered by a calligrapher, or printed—not only entices guests, it also lets them know what to expect so they can pace their appetites, avoid ingredients they don't care for, and anticipate what silverware to use for each course.

Menu

Caviar and smoked salmon

Roast Beef and Yorkshire pudding

Roasted vegetables

Horseradish cream sauce

Bûche de Noël

Cinnamon ice cream

Tropical Idyll

My family has been going to Palm Beach to enjoy a respite from New York winters since I was a baby. We would visit my grandparents, who liked to spend the winter in Florida and had a house there. Eventually Estée purchased the Mediterranean Revival house next door for my parents. They have echoed much of Estée's style in this house, including re-creating her lacy wrought-iron patio furniture and sky-blue Florida room. My whole family often comes down over New Year's, and now my children love it as much as I do.

My mother hosts a formal sit-down dinner on New Year's Eve for fifty, with everyone in black tie, but we also enjoy casual lunches in our bathing suits, sitting on the porch overlooking the ocean. I celebrated my fortieth birthday here with a group of close friends with a stone crab dinner on the terrace. There is no formal dining room in this house because we eat outside as much as possible. Instead, the large, pale pink living room has a dining table at one end where we can eat when it's too chilly outside. Life is generally much more relaxed here, and entertaining can be as effortless as inviting friends over for a piña colada or rum punch by the pool. Vibrant tropical flowers such as orchids, bougainvillea, and frangipani lend not only color but fragrance to the garden and my table settings. My mother might use just a big bowl of green coconuts (the tropical equivalent of her green apples) as a simple, fresh centerpiece. Everything is colorful, light, and easygoing, which is what makes it so appealing for entertaining or simply relaxing.

OPPOSITE: The expanse of tranquil blue sea and green grass dotted with palm trees is the definition of relaxation. Life here is about going barefoot, swimming, and sunning. Entertaining is as casual as a mojito by the pool and occasionally as formal as my mother's black-tie New Year's Eve dinner.

ABOVE: Our family at my grandparents' Palm Beach house in the 1970s, with Estée and Joseph at each side, and me in my father's lap, third from left. OPPOSITE: Our 1940s-style wrought-iron patio furniture is just like my grandmother's. Verdant trees, palms, and tropical flowers enclosed by stucco walls create the feeling of a secret garden. FOLLOWING PAGES: Lounge chairs lined up by the pool offer a perfect spot to have drinks with friends or just relax with a great novel.

LOCAL COLOR

Wherever I am, I like to take advantage of the local cuisine, flowers, style, and traditions to enhance my entertaining.

• In Palm Beach, for me, that means key lime pies, stone crab, chocolate-covered coconut patties, cheese puffs, and piña coladas.

• In New York, you can get almost any kind of food, but out-of-town guests enjoy having fresh bagels and lox for breakfast, and I might make my chicken hash recipe, inspired by the one served at the 21 Club, or share our latest local find among the vast melting pot of delicacies New York has to offer.

• When we are out at the beach, it would be a crime not to take advantage of the freshly caught fish and lobster (and lobster rolls); the bounty of fresh corn, tomatoes, and vegetables at the local farm stands and in our own garden; and irresistible homemade ice cream.

• In the Rocky Mountains, we tend to serve hearty fare, like delicious steak and lamb, along with local craft brews.

• Wherever you are, be sure to share the local treasures and freshest seasonal offerings with your guests. It may seem old hat to you, but it will impart a sense of place and your region's unique flavors and culture to your visitors.

OPPOSITE: A mouthwatering frozen piña colada on a hot day, garnished with fresh mint and orange slices, is virtually irresistible. Even poolside, I like to add pretty flowers like these tender orchids, shells I've collected, and raffia accessories to make the moment special.

Resources

TABLETOP: CHINA, GLASSWARE & MORE

AERIN
Everything I love most is represented in our beautifully designed collections of tabletop, entertaining accessories, barware, candles, and more.
aerin.com

7 Newtown Lane
East Hampton, NY 11937
631-527-5517

83 Main Street
Southampton, NY 11968
631-353-3773

33 Via Mizner
Palm Beach, FL 33480
561-623-0906

See aerin.com for additional retailers

Bergdorf Goodman
Bergdorf's has always been one of my favorite New York stores for plates and glassware. I especially love the home floor. They source artisans from all over the world and their Christmas selection is not to be missed.

754 Fifth Avenue
New York, NY 10019
bergdorfgoodman.com

James Robinson
James Robinson has the most beautiful silver, antique porcelain, and glassware. I registered for my wedding at James Robinson when I was twenty-four years old and to this day it's my choice for baby gifts and fine silver.

480 Park Avenue
New York, NY 10022
212-752-6166
jrobinson.com

La Tuile à Loup
This impeccably curated ceramics store in the Quartier Latin is not to be missed. Owner Eric Goujou travels all over France to find the best artisanal pottery, including distinctive Provençal aptware, marbleware, and more.

35 rue Daubenton
75005 Paris, France
latuilealoup.com

March
This is my favorite home store in San Francisco, a must-visit known for its modern spatterware ceramics, glassware, and unique finds.

3075 Sacramento Street
San Francisco, CA 94115
415-931-7433
marchsf.com

Penny Morrison
I always try to visit this special store when I'm in London. Penny's shop is a magical visual paradise. From her custom tableware and beautifully hued candles to her elegant fabrics, I love her sensibility and edit.

9 Langton Street
Chelsea, London, United Kingdom
SW10 0JL
pennymorrison.com

Scully & Scully
This is a Park Avenue institution for timeless, elegant pieces. Perfect for when you are missing that last finishing piece, like place mats or a silver Buccellati candy bowl.

504 Park Avenue
New York, NY 10022
212-755-2590
scullyandscully.com

Williams Sonoma
Williams Sonoma shares my sense of style and passion for impeccable design, which is why it has always been a go-to destination for anything I may need in my kitchen and home.
williams-sonoma.com

HOME FURNISHINGS

The Shade Store
The AERIN collection for The Shade Store offers tonal block prints and florals. Their expansive offerings and expertise make them a great source for window coverings.
theshadestore.com

Visual Comfort
Visual Comfort and AERIN have partnered to create an in-depth lighting collection that I love. This well-crafted, uniquely designed lighting fills many rooms in my home.
visualcomfort.com

TABLE LINENS & FABRICS

Carolina Irving Textiles
Carolina is one of my favorite designers for fabric and tabletop.
carolinairvingtextiles.com

D. Porthault
Porthault is a pattern-lover's paradise. They're known for their classic heart pattern but I've always loved their florals—the more, the better—in a beautiful palette that can be mixed and matched.

470 Park Avenue
New York, NY 10022
& additional locations
dporthaultparis.com

Fortuny
This classic Italian fabric house produces the most exquisite designs.

979 Third Avenue
Suite 1632
New York, NY 10022
212-753-7153
fortuny.com

Lee Jofa
Our wonderful fabric partner is the source
for an amazing array of fabrics and rugs,
from classic to modern.

AERIN fabrics for Lee Jofa to the trade
kravet.com

Leontine Linens
Custom monogrammed table linens,
as well as bed linens, towels,
and travel accessories, with old-school
charm and elegance.

3806 Magazine Street #3
New Orleans, LA 70115
504-899-7833
leontinelinens.com

Lori Jayne
My go-to for tabletop, towels, and
linens in Palm Beach. Their beautiful
monogramming makes a great gift
for someone special.

304 S. County Road
Palm Beach, FL 33480
561-855-4290
lorijayne.com

FLORAL DESIGN

Bridgehampton Florist
The flower arrangements and plants from
my favorite florist on Long Island always
look hand-done and special.

2400 Montauk Highway
Bridgehampton, NY 11932
631-537-7766
thebridgehamptonflorist.com

Raúl Àvila
This incredibly talented event planner and
floral designer in New York City worked
on my wedding many years ago and I
still rely on him for personal flowers as
well as for special events.

20 West 22nd Street, Suite 1012
New York, NY 10010
212-242-7673

Zezé
Bringing a Brazilian flair to New York
City, Zezé is a favorite for orchids,
unique plants, flowers, and special gifts.

938 First Avenue
New York, NY 10022
212-753-7767

INVITATIONS, MENUS & PLACE CARDS

Bernard Maisner
Custom calligraphy that looks like
a work of art.
bernardmaisner.com

Happy Menocal
Custom-painted watercolor illustrations for
invitations and menus; her work has a
whimsical flair that never disappoints.
happymenocal.com

Kinship Press
This talented sister duo creates
custom watercolors for invitations,
menus, and more.
kinship-press.com

PARTY DECORATIONS

Brooklyn Balloon Company
Balloon art masterpieces that you'll never
want to take down.
brooklynballooncompany.com

Fiona Leahy Design
My favorite English event planner
specializes in whimsical table
designs and offers wonderful
custom Christmas crackers.
fionaleahy.com

Meri Meri
Who says delightful paper and party
goods are only for children?
merimeri.com for retailers or orders

CAKES, CANDY & FOOD

Edelweiss
This chocolate shop is a Beverly
Hills tradition that offers always-
tasteful hostess gifts.

444 N. Canon Drive
Beverly Hills, CA 90210
310-275-0341
edelweisschocolates.com

Lael Cakes
Brooklyn-based Emily Lael Aumiller's
custom gluten-free, vegan,
and dairy-optional cakes are
both delectable and exquisite.
laelcakes.com

Magnolia Bakery
I love their old-fashioned cupcakes
and cakes with buttercream flowers
or colorful confetti.
magnoliabakery.com

Sockerbit
This Swedish company's candy is as fun
to look at as it is delicious. The oversize
red gummy hearts are a personal favorite.

89 Christopher Street
New York, NY 10014
212-206-8170
sockerbit.com

Teuscher
They're known for their famous dark
champagne truffles, but their decorative
boxes are as enticing as the chocolates.
teuscher.com

William Poll
This specialty food shop is many a New
York hostess's secret source, with the best
dips, homemade chips, frozen soufflés,
and magical gingerbread houses.

1051 Lexington Avenue
New York, NY 10021
212-288-0501
williampoll.com

4 Mr. Huckue
2 Mrs. Brokaw
Mr. Rome
1 Countess Cicogna
3

6 Mrs. Shaw
8 Mr. Gustal
10 Mrs. de Heeren
12 Mr. Whitley
14 Countess Cicogna
16 Ambassador Rifai
18 Mrs. de Pinies
20 Mr. Lauder
22 Mrs. Van der Kemp
24 Mr. Sarnoff
26 Mrs. Liberman
28 Baron Radowitz
30 Mrs. Sarnoff
32 Mr. Smith
34 Mrs. Fondaras

5 Zar De Houya
7 Mrs. Ford
9 Mr. Clarkson
11 Mrs. Guest
13 Count Vega del Ren
15 Mrs. Melle
17 Mr. Van der Kemp
19 Mrs. Lauder
21 Ambassador de Pinies
23 Mrs. Patiño
25 Mr. Liberman
27 Mrs. Wyatt
29 Mr. Kricker
31 Mrs. Desmarais
Mr. Carr
35 Mrs. Sadleman

36 Mr. Brokaw
38 Countess Cittadini
37 Mr. Van Miersse

LEFT: In memory of Henry, my parents' favorite dog, and my favorite guest at any party. We miss you so much. OPPOSITE: One of Estée's seating charts for a formal dinner. Small strips of paper with the names of her guests could be rearranged until she was happy with the placement.

ACKNOWLEDGMENTS

I am so grateful for the amazing and talented team that worked with me to bring this book to life: photographer Simon Upton, whose photographs perfectly captured my ideas and sensibility; Doug Turshen for sharing his vision with me and the great art direction (no matter how many times I decided to add new ideas); my publisher, Rizzoli, and Charles Miers and Aliza Fogelson, whose thoughtfulness and dedication to each and every detail guided me along the way; and Jill Simpson, who graciously put my ideas on paper and authentically told my story. And a special thank you to Mary O'Neil, whose calm demeanor and masterful organization guaranteed that everything from photo shoots to text changes ran smoothly and efficiently.

Thank you to my mother, Jo Carole Lauder, for teaching me so much about entertaining, style, life, and motherhood. And to my grandmother Estée for being an incredible mentor in both business and personal ventures.

I am so appreciative of the contributors who participated and were so supportive throughout the process. To Maria Hummer-Tuttle, Daniel Romualdez, and Caroline Sieber von Westenholz: you are all such an inspiration to me and I am honored to share your entertaining styles. Thank you to Raúl Àvila, Zezé Calvo, and Michael Grimm, each of whose incredible taste in flowers is evident on every page. Finally, thank you to Alexa Rodulfo for creating magic on countless shoots, and chef Josh Page, for curating beautiful and delicious presentations.

PHOTOGRAPHY CREDITS

All photography by Simon Upton except as follows:

Björn Wallander/OTTO: 183, 187

Claiborne Swanson Frank: 91

Craig McDean: 172

Elizabeth Kuhner Archives, care of
Kate Kuhner Photography: 230

Francesco Lagnese: 195, 213

François Halard: 184–85, 188–89

Fred J. Maroon: 13

Isabel Parra: Endpapers, 10, 238

Jenna Bascom Photography: 57–67

Joe Schildhorn/BFA.com: 40

Lindsay Stall: 173–79

Mark Lund: 70–73, 78–79, 235

Mary Hilliard Photography: 8

Maya Myers Photography: 112–13, 115–25, 128, 129

Oberto Gili, Architectural Digest © Condé Nast:
229, 231, 232–33

Photo by EVAAN: 69

Robert Fairer: 204–11

Roger Davies: 110, 126–27

Silja Magg: 21, 92–95, 130, 214–15

Tawni Bannister: 217

ARTWORK CREDITS

Pages 5, 213, 214–15, 221: Painting by Lucio Fontana

Pages 44, 46–47, 149, 222–23: Artworks by Jean Dubuffet

Page 57: Framed flower photograph by Paul Lange

Pages 76–77: Woodcut by Robert Mangold

Pages 104–105: Botanical engraving by Georg Ehret

Pages 130, 202 (top): Drawing by Edgar Degas

Page 133, 134, 135, 137: Beauvais tapestry,
first half of the eighteenth century

Page 139: Work on paper by Franz Kline (top), screenprint
by Cy Twombly (center), drawing by Pablo Picasso (bottom),
sculpture by Jean Arp

Pages 140–41: Screenprint by Cy Twombly (top), drawing
by Pablo Picasso (bottom), sculpture by Jean Arp

Page 142: Artwork by Yves Klein

Page 147: Artwork by Mark Rothko

Pages 157, 161: Painting by Ellsworth Kelly

Pages 158–59: Artworks by Ellsworth Kelly,
sculpture by Constantin Brancusi

Pages 162–63: Painting by Brice Marden

Page 164: Painting by Robert Ryman (above), painting by
Franz Kline (below), potato sculpture by Claes Oldenburg
atop an early nineteenth-century American sideboard
by John and Thomas Seymour

Pages 197, 198–99: Work on paper by Richard Serra,
painting by Jacob Jordaens

Page 202 (top): Drawing by Paul Cézanne

First published in the United States of America in
2020 by
Rizzoli International Publications, Inc.
300 Park Avenue South
New York, NY 10010
www.rizzoliusa.com

Copyright © 2020 AERIN LLC
Principal photography © 2020 Simon Upton
Additional photography and artwork credits
appear above.

Publisher: Charles Miers
Editor: Aliza Fogelson
Design: Doug Turshen and Steve Turner
Production Manager: Colin Hough Trapp
Managing Editor: Lynn Scrabis

Printed in Italy

2022 2023 2024 / 10 9 8 7 6

ISBN: 978-0-8478-6752-3
Library of Congress Control Number: 2020935909

Visit us online:
Facebook.com/RizzoliNewYork
Twitter: @Rizzoli_Books
Instagram.com/RizzoliBooks
Pinterest.com/RizzoliBooks
Youtube.com/user/RizzoliNY
issuu.com/Rizzoli